LEAD
TO SUCCEED

Also by Michael Beer:
The Joy of Selling

LEAD
TO SUCCEED

Studies in Managing People

MICHAEL BEER

MERCURY

First published in January 1989
by the Mercury Books Division of
W. H. Allen & Co. Plc
Sekforde House, 175–9 St John Street, London EC1V 4LL
Published in paperback 1990

Set in Palatino by Input Typesetting Ltd, London
Printed and bound in Great Britain by
Mackays of Chatham PLC, Chatham, Kent.

British Library Cataloguing in Publication Data

Beer, Michael
    Lead to succeed.
    1. Personnel management – Case studies
    I. Title
    658.3'00722

ISBN 1–85252–032–9

Contents

1

INTRODUCTION

What is a Manager?

A manager is someone who manages people.

If you are a manager – really a manager, not merely someone who carries the title – then you manage people.

If you are in charge of machines in a factory, figures on paper or stores in a warehouse then you are not a manager. These things – machines, figures, stores – don't have to be managed. They are not doing anything, they are simply sitting there. They may have to be counted or arranged or guarded or cleaned or protected or distributed or repaired, but they don't need to be *managed*.

People, only people, need to be managed, and only someone in charge of people is truly a manager.

If you are a manager then you are involved with people every day of your working life. You have meetings, interviews, chats and conferences with them. During these encounters you use words to express ideas in order to praise, teach, discipline, explore, train and persuade. Your competence as a manager depends largely on how well you use the words, how well you express the ideas.

As far as your job relates to people there are two basic aspects, only one of which is managing people. The other is the setting out of policies and procedures, limits of authority and responsibility, job specifications, and targets and goals.

This book is concerned with the people part of your job, not the policy part. We are presuming that you have set out the standards you expect from your people. Now comes the second part of your job; now you have to see that the standards are met and maintained, that the job is being done.

That is what this book is about.

One of the things which makes the job of a manager so tricky is that it is rather like having a baby, in that you can't do a test run on it. Every time you do it, it's for real, and you have to get it right that time. It's much easier when you are working with things rather than people; for instance, if you get a trial balance wrong you tear it up and do it over, if you do a stock count badly you have only wasted some time. But screw up on a management undertaking and you can't press the CLEAR button and start again.

WHAT WE ARE GOING TO DO

In the examples which fill the pages of this book we shall be examining many of the people problems which face a manager, and the people decisions which a manager makes. We shall see how company rules and strategies, when they are brought to bear on people with varied backgrounds, cultures and personalities, can often create serious conflict. We shall recognise that people problems can often arise from impatience, fear, misunderstanding, lack of direction, or poor self-motivation.

HOW WE ARE GOING TO DO IT

This book uses the case study method to show how people manage and are managed. To be precise, some of the scenarios are case *studies*, where the situation has been invented in order to make a point; some are case *histories*, which actually happened. By no means all the stories have a happy ending - this is as much a 'How Not To' book as it is a 'How To'. You will watch as managers painstakingly try to put some spine into a timid subordinate, ruthlessly cut a rebel down to size, tactfully handle a thorny but valuable old stager, use detective work to discover the real crime, and deal with the problem of a sudden promotion over their mates.

In the case method you will be able to sit in unobserved while the managers and their men and women play out the drama. From time to time we shall stop the action and ask: 'How's it going so far? Is the manager handling the problem effectively? What other options does he have?' We shall therefore have one priceless advantage which is denied any manager; we *can* press the CLEAR button, we can go back and try it another way, and ask if that way would work better.

ENJOY!

You have one of the most fascinating and exciting jobs in the world; you manage people. If your job is so interesting then anything written about it had better be just as interesting. I expect you to learn from this book, but I also expect you to find it to be absorbing, interesting and even exciting. If you don't find it so then I shall have failed.

Let's see.

2

A Manager for all seasons

A good manager is for all seasons, and we shall look at managers in all their seasons. We shall see them tossing bouquets and brickbats, handing out laurel wreaths and wielding a terrible swift sword, as the occasion requires.

Does this mean that the good manager has to be a chameleon, changing colour to suit every condition he finds himself in? Yes and no. He is not a hypocrite, changing masks for each occasion he has to become involved in. He is himself at all times, but he does show different facets of his character in order to handle different people in different situations.

What's the difference? Putting on different masks, displaying different facets of oneself – it's all hypocrisy, isn't it, if we are not showing our true colours? Well, what is hypocrisy? The dictionary defines it as: 'The practice of professing standards or beliefs contrary to one's real character or behaviour.' If you don't like the sound of that then flip the pages back to the definition of Adaptation: 'Changing to suit a different purpose or condition.' Sounds much better, until you realise that they are both saying pretty much the same thing.

Whatever you like to call it, if you are to become an effective manager you are going to have to modify, change or adapt your 'natural' character to suit different purposes or conditions. For instance you may be very direct, down-to-earth and plain-spoken by nature and temperament, but while this style may be excellent in some situations it could be a disaster when dealing, for instance, with some Middle or Far Eastern peoples, where the direct approach would set any meeting of minds back ten years.

The good manager is one for all seasons. This actually happened:

A sales manager had tried for a long time – much too long – to get one of his salesmen to conform to the standards set out for the sales team. The man had potential, no doubt about that, but as for his toeing the line in matters of paperwork, after-sales service, punctuality, handling customer complaints and the scores of small things that add up to good work – no amount of reprimanding, correcting, cajoling or instructing seemed to have any effect.

Eventually the manager decided to stop the rot once and for all. He summoned the salesman to a meeting in his office and, while he waited for the salesman, the manager paged through the salesman's file. As he counted the times he had tried to straighten out the salesman's behaviour, and the times that had had no effect, the manager found himself getting more and more heated until he was as furious as he could ever remember being. When the salesman walked in after a perfunctory tap on the door he was ready for him.

The salesman threw himself casually into a chair.

'What's the problem, chief?' he asked, pulling out a cigarette.

'Who gave you permission to sit down in this office? Stand up! No smoking!' His manager's tone could have been used to freeze liquid nitrogen. The salesman's face lost all its colour; never had the chief spoken to him like that before. He sat as though turned to stone.

'Did you hear me? You stand until I tell you to sit!' He almost ruptured himself getting to his feet. The manager threw the salesman's file at him. 'Read that. Read every page of it, right this minute.' The salesman opened his mouth. 'Shut up and read it!'

The salesman read through the list of his deficiencies, short-comings and sins. When he had turned the last page his manager said, and his words could have been bitten off steel plate: 'Now you listen to me, you bastard. I am going to get thirty perfect days from you. For the next thirty days you are going to be the thirteenth Apostle. If I get one complaint from a customer, if you submit one form just five minutes late, if you are one unit short of your quota, you are fired. No matter what goes wrong in your territory I am automatically going to blame you for it. One wrong shipment, one bad debt, one scratch on your car – I am going to assume that it's your fault and fire you so fast that you won't hit ground until you are sixty feet away. In thirty days I want you back in this office, clean, pure and smelling like a rose. Now get out of here.'

When the salesman had left, the manager sat there with his mouth dry, his hands shaking and his heart pounding in his chest. That simply was not him talking, you see. He had always had an easy, informal relationship with his team, he was on a first-name basis with them, he ran his show in a very permissive atmosphere.

Here he was stepping right out of character and it was so unexpected that it had profoundly shaken both the salesman and the manager himself. Word got round the office very quickly that the boss had suddenly and inexplicably changed from Mary Poppins to Ivan the Terrible, and everyone trod very carefully for the next few days.

One month later the salesman came back as ordered. In that time he had indeed conducted himself without spot or blemish. For once he had produced a perfect month. This time the manager had himself well under control. He invited the salesman to sit – he had been standing practically to attention – and he spoke quietly.

'Very well, you have given me thirty perfect days. Good. You are not off the hook yet and you won't be until I say so, but you are thirty days further away from losing your job. I want thirty more days, exactly as good as the ones you have just delivered. That's all.'

Two weeks later the salesman's wife came to see the manager. She had tears in her eyes and her voice shook with emotion as she thanked him for, as she put it, saving her husband from drifting into failure. Apparently from the date of that first interview the salesman had changed his attitude towards his job, himself, his direction in life and even, his wife insisted, towards his marriage. 'He's a different man,' she said, 'And it's thanks to you. When you gave him hell that day it was just what he needed. Thank you, thank you!' She pushed a little packet at the manager and ducked out of his office. The packet contained a silver cigarette lighter and a card saying 'Thank you' and her name.

As it happens, I was the manager. I didn't have to tell that since the story makes its point without that piece of information, and I mention it only because I know myself and I know that normally I don't come within a million miles of acting like that. That steely-eyed tyrant spitting out venom *was not Michael Beer*. I put on an entirely new mask for that occasion. I didn't turn a new facet of myself to the light because I don't have that facet in my make-up. I *assumed* that character just as one puts on a different colour shirt.

The purpose of that story is not to demonstrate my skill in handling a particular person. Who knows? The salesman's reaction could have been: 'Who do you think you're talking to? I quit, and you can go to hell!' – In which case I would have failed. No, I gave that example only to show you that if you are to succeed as a manager you are going to have to 'change to suit a different purpose or condition', as the definiton of 'Adapt' goes.

Here's a thought to chew on:

> You don't have problems with bad people – you have problems with good people who have problems.

It's true. Find a really bad egg in the nest and what do you do? You throw it out, that's what. Buy a packet of oranges and find a squishy one, no problem – get rid of it. The really bad people don't present a problem, you merely fire them. It is true that this action may produce secondary problems in that you now have to replace the one you got rid of (always assuming that he left a vacancy, that is). Also it does sometimes happen that when a team-member is fired it can affect the morale of the rest of the team. These are possible results of firing the bad one, but the bad one is no longer a problem.

The good one with the problem? *He's* the one who gives you the headache. You don't want to get rid of him, he's too good to lose, but he does have a problem and while he has it you are not getting full value from his services. This is where you show your worth as a manager.

If another analogy is necessary, look at the job of the surgeon who is presented with the case of a factory worker who has suffered a horrific accident. His hand has been crushed in a machine. The surgeon brings all his expertise and experience to his careful and thorough examination of the hand. Reluctantly he decides that the injury is too severe; the hand can under no circumstances be saved and amputation is necessary. In this case the youngest trainee surgeon would be able to do the job of amputating and neatly sewing up the stump. No problem, the case was too bad.

But let us say that after the examination the surgeon decides that, yes, the hand can be saved. There is just sufficient bone, tendon and tissue still undamaged to make a repair possible. *Now* he has the problem of doing the job, and it will require all his skill.

No, you have no problem with the bad ones, only with the good ones who have problems.

Those are the ones we are about to examine in this book.

3

The would-be executive

Charlie Bigshot could fill his manager's chair tomorrow – and do a better job than his manager, according to him. He doesn't come right out and say so, but that's obviously the way he thinks and certainly the way he acts. He dominates sales meetings to the extent that a bystander would wonder who was in charge – Charlie or his boss. He's a good talker, too, and what he says is usually worth listening to. He tends to come into his manager's office, drape himself over the desk and discuss sales strategy as though between equals.

Charlie's sales figures have always been in the top twenty per cent of the sales chart. He is well-educated, dresses quietly and expensively, is a member of two sports clubs and is a competent show-jumper and rally driver. He married into money and his wife's picture appears in the society pages. Most of the sales team look up to him and respect his ideas.

Charlie has become touchy and impatient lately and the reason is not far to seek; his manager seems glued to his chair and there is no obvious way for

Charlie to take it over, nor is there any other apparent opening for him on the executive ladder. His manager has decided that things can't go on as they are and that the time has come for a clearing of the air. He has asked Charlie to come and see him in his office.

Charlie strides in and starts talking without greeting Mac, his manager:

Charlie: Mac, I have just come from Despatch. Would you believe it, old Arthur was about to send out that order of Model 77's to Johnson & Fripp without the heavy-duty filters! I have told him before *never* to send any units to J & F without heavy-duty filters.

Mac: Did Johnson & Fripp order the heavy-duty filters?

Charlie: No, but if you could see the conditions those 77's have to work in you'd realise–

Mac: All right. That's not what I want to talk about.

Charlie: But that's important, Mac. Perhaps you should consider that old Arthur is getting past it. I know that he reports to Production, but if you told Hopkins–

Mac: Charlie! I don't want to talk about Arthur. I want to talk about you. Sit down.

Charlie: What about me?

Mac: Well, what about you? You've been acting up lately. What is the matter?

Charlie: Acting up? What is that supposed to mean, acting up?

18

Mac: I mean that you have been upsetting people. You didn't have to tell me that you had just come from Despatch. I have just had a call from Arthur, complaining that you bawled him out in front of his own men.

Charlie: I didn't bawl him out, for God's sake–

Mac: Wait a minute. Yesterday Miss Hudson walked in here and said that you had had one of her girls in tears. You can't just barge into the typing pool and terrorise junior typists, damn it!

Charlie: Now, hang on there, Mac. That girl made three stupid mistakes in the quotation for Pratt Construction. That order could be worth–

Mac: Will you shut up and listen to me? (Charlie clamps his mouth closed and stares at the window. Mac continues quietly.) What's happened, Charlie? You don't usually do the sort of things you are doing now. You get on well with people. You have the respect and liking of the internal staff – or you did have. Now suddenly I'm getting stories and complaints about you. (Charlie remains silent.) There's another thing. This is mid-September. By now your sales figures should be showing an upswing for the seasonal rise; yours are slightly down if anything. When I see this happening to one of my best salesmen I begin to worry. (He puts some warmth into his voice.) Hey, open up, Charlie. What's going on? Perhaps I can help. (Charlie remains unbending, remote. Mac opens his mouth to speak and closes it again. At last Charlie sighs, rubs his eyes with the heels of his hands and turns to face Mac.)

Charlie: Mac, the only way you can help me is by dying.

Mac: Wha-a-at?

Charlie: Die, resign, or emigrate (he leans forward and puts his fists on the desk). Mac, The only thing wrong with me is that I am sitting on the wrong side of this desk. I want your job, Mac. I'm ready for it and I know I can do it. You do a good job, I'm not saying anything about the way you handle the administrative side of the job, but I know that I could do that part of it as well as you could. As for the personal side of it–

Mac: You could do that part better than I could, is that it?

Charlie: Mac, don't get upset, but yes, I think I handle people well. It's one of my strengths.

Mac: As you handled Arthur this morning and Evelyn yesterday (He puts his hands up quickly). All right, that was uncalled for. Charlie, let's talk about this. I can understand that you would like to move up, of course–

Charlie: Mac, it's not a question of what I would like. It's what I deserve! Look at my record in this company; I have opened up more new accounts than any single salesman. I turned the North-Eastern territory from a loser to a money-spinner in eighteen months. I put the Model D–55 on the market against the stiffest opposition from the Midas Corporation. I raised–

Mac: Enough, Charlie! I know your record as well as you do. You don't have to convince me that you can sell. But that's just the point, isn't it? You are a good salesman. Who says you can be a good manager? You haven't any management experience.

Charlie (slapping the desk): And just how am I supposed to get management experience sitting on my arse in a sales territory? (He points an accusing finger.) How much management experience did you have before they promoted you from the sales team?

Mac: Okay, you may be right. But what do you expect me to do, Charlie? Apart from dying, resigning or emigrating, that is? I can't very well go to Cookson and tell him to die, resign or emigrate so that I can have his job because you want mine.

Charlie: So there's really only one thing for me to do, isn't there?

Mac: Such as what?

Charlie: Leave the company, of course. Quit my job.

Mac: Oh, nonsense. You don't mean that.

Charlie (Kicks his chair back and stands up): Don't I? Don't I? What else can I do? Cookson is set in his job and is too young to retire. You can't move up except into Cookson's job, and until you move there is no opening for me. How do you think my wife likes it when her friends ask her if I'm still a rep? In less than two years I'll be thirty. Shall I hang around here just so that I can get into the Guinness Book of Records as the oldest living salesman?

Let's stop there and see where we are. We have a good man here and he has a very serious problem. It is not merely a question of blocked promotion; it goes a lot deeper than that. We get a taste of a personal problem here too. He is getting headwind from his socialite wife that she would like an executive as a husband instead of a 'rep'. Also, Charlie is going through some sort of crisis of his very own. His mention of his age indicates that he feels the years are passing and are being charged to his account.

You are Mac. At this point, what would you do? Here are some options, and let us spread our net as wide as we can. We want to save Charlie if at all possible:

1. Take the problem to Cookson, your boss. Isn't it his job to make sure that there are positions in the company so that we can make the best use of people like Charlie?

2. Create a position for Charlie. Call him 'Key Accounts Supervisor' or 'Field Manager' – whatever. His actual job responsibilities don't have to change and it will at least help get his wife off his case.

3. Tell him that you agree with him that there is no slot for him, now or in the foreseeable future, and if he feels he has to go, then so be it and the best of luck in whatever job he finds for himself.

4. Tell him that twenty-eight years old is hardly in the geriatric league, and that a little patience is in order.

5. Tell him that you believe his future is in selling, not in management, and that he is making a very good living at the moment and that there is nothing wrong with being a salesman.

6. Tell him to stop whining, stop bothering you and, most important, stop treading on people's toes, or you will really give him something to whine about.

Do we like any of these? Comments, please, on each of the above:

1. Are you going to run to Papa every time you can't do your homework? This is *your* problem.

2. Charlie is not a stupid person. He will surely see that you are giving him a corporal's stripes while he is still doing a private's job.

3. Telling him to like it or lump it is a nice, simple way to get rid of the problem – and, probably, get rid of Charlie, too.

4. When you are twenty-eight years old and things are not happening as fast as you want them to, it can seem to be a very great age.

5. Telling him that there is nothing wrong with being a salesman (when you are nicely ensconced in a manager's job) is not very tactful and will not go down very well with Charlie. He already sees you as part of the problem.

6. Sure, let's slap him down. Then he will leave the company and we can get on with what ever it was we were doing before he came in and bothered us.

None of these options is very attractive, is it? Perhaps we should stop looking at things we could say to him and instead examine the facts. They are these:

- Is he a good man? Yes, he is one of the best.

- But his record of competence is in the field of selling, not of management. Yes, but in his attitude, his behaviour (before he became so tetchy), the way that others regard him, there are strong indications that he could be a good leader.

- Do we therefore wish if at all possible to keep him,

23

both for his present sales ability and for his future potential as a manager? No question about that, certainly.

- Is there any way that we can give him the promotion which he so ardently desires and, to be honest, probably deserves? No.

- Will he be prepared to carry on in his present job with no chance of promotion? No.

- Then how on earth are we going to keep him? We are probably not going to be able to keep him. Somehow, somewhere along the line, things went wrong, and we are going to lose one of our best salesmen; a man who almost certainly has management potential.

Is there any way we could have foreseen this problem and avoided it? This was a small company, without divisions, branches, departments or sections spread all over the place. In such a company it would not have been difficult to give Charlie a position which would have provided him with the authority (and the title and status) which he wanted. He would have been satisfied and we would have retained the services of a good man. In that sort of horizontal organisation this is done all the time, and it is one of the reasons that people join a company with a wide range of product divisions and a national or international spread.

Charlie is with a relatively small and highly special-ised company. When we say small, it is in fact one of the leaders in its field, but it is an outfit without a large work-force. (The market leader in gas-permeable contact lenses does not have the size of staff that the market leader in toothpaste has.)

Perhaps on second thoughts Mac *should* have taken the problem to Cookson, his boss? Not so much to help with Charlie's situation as to point out the likelihood of this sort of thing happening again, and to ask what could be done to avoid losing more people as good as Charlie in future?

Anyway, this is what happened. Mac said something along these lines:

Charlie, I hear you. It's only natural that you should want to look to your future. Sometimes when we do this the future seems to be blurred. We can't see ahead as clearly as we would like to and it's a worrying thing. Now, it looks to you as though the way up in this company is through the job that I am holding at this moment. In fact, this may not be true. Right now there is no other path, but remember this, Charlie; this is a growth company. Look back over the past four years and you will realise that in that time we have grown by over 100 per cent. When you came to us four years ago we had a sales force of myself and three salesmen. Now we have seven. If we keep on like this – and there's no reason why we shouldn't, with the expansion of our product range – then it won't be all that long before we have to split the sales force into two. That means another management job opening up. Later we shall probably need area supervisors at the first line and a general sales manager at the senior level. Nobody can promise that all this will happen, Charlie, but doesn't it seem highly likely?

When it happens, who do you think will be the ones considered for the new jobs? They will be those with good, solid track records – the sort of record that you are building up right now.

As I say, no promises because nobody can predict

the future with certainty. But think about it, Charlie. Give it a lot of thought, talk to Angela about it, walk around it before you make any decision. And let's talk like this more often.

Well, Charlie chewed it over and came back a few days later to say that he had decided to hang on and see what happened. Which sounds as though Mac had neatly and effectively solved the problem, until we look eight months ahead and see that Charlie resigned, finally and definitely, and refused even to discuss it with his manager or anyone else.

WHAT COULD HAVE BEEN DONE?

Of the meeting between Charlie and his manager there probably isn't much to say. Mac could have handled it more skilfully perhaps, but even we, sitting on the sidelines, could find little comfort in any of the alternatives we offered him.

The truth is that there is little that Mac could have done in the interview, because the situation was not one that could have been solved *at his level of authority*. At a higher level, had Mac taken it to Cookson, it *might* have been handled in various exotic ways denied to a first-line manager such as Mac. Charlie could have been sent to the factory for intensive product training, he could have been transferred to a branch in another city (or even another country), he might have been encouraged to take a part-time MBA course at the company's expense. In the rarified air of the bosses' bosses, many things are possible. Whether they would work is another thing again.

The problem of Charlie, when stripped down to

the bone, is the problem of too many Indians wanting to become Chiefs – and, in some cases, deserving the job. It is one of the most common causes of staff turnover. Your worker may look as though he is happy in his job and willing to soldier on at it indefinitely, but what you don't know is that tucked away in his bottom drawer is a *time-table*. This is a fascinating document, known only to himself and his wife. The first date on it is the day he left school, and the last date says next to it: 'Retire from Board of Directors – go on world cruise'.

The problem is that he is already behind schedule. His time-table states that he should have become a supervisor last year, but here he is still a clerk in the payroll department. You might be astonished to learn how many workers in your hive know exactly to the day just when they will become Queen Bee.

In the case of our worker who has himself down for a supervisor's position, and who is already eighteen months late for it, one of two things can happen. He can revise his time-table, recognising that he was a little optimistic about the rate of promotion; or he can become more and more unsatisfied and frustrated until his work begins to suffer or he decides to leave this company, where his merit is not being awarded as it deserves, and seek his fortune elsewhere.

Accept the existence of the time-table. It may not be written down on paper, but it is in the minds of every worker on your team. Next year I should make foreman. In three years I want to be second-in-command of the industrial department. By the time I'm thirty I shall be ready for the job of textile buyer, and they had better give it to me or I'll know the reason why.

The time-table may be a very flexible thing – no

more than a rather vague feeling that every year or so he needs to see that he has made some sort of progress. Or it may be a hard-and-fast list with each step up carved in stone with the exact date and time. Either way it exists, and we ignore it at our peril.

Look, it's a *good* thing. Anyone who has no picture in his mind of where he wants to go, how long it will take him to get there and what path he will choose along the route is not going *anywhere*, and is that the sort of person you want working for you? Perhaps it is. Perhaps all you think you need are those dozen or so heads submissively bent over their ledgers or milling machines or word-processors, unchanging from year to year except that they grow greyer or balder as time goes by. There are not many of those around these days and you won't get much from them except the absolute basic requirements of the job. Everyone else has a time-table. You have one, don't you? Of course you do, and if anything happened to throw it out of kilter you would become worried, irritated and apprehensive. Your work would probably suffer. Your relations with people would worsen. You would want your manager to realise that you have a time-table.

Just as Charlie did.

With Charlie it should have been recognised long ago that anyone with his background, his performance record and his high-profile personality would have a clearly-defined time-table. It should have been seen four years ago when he joined the company that Mac would end up having exactly the sort of confrontation that he did. The moment Charlie was hired the seeds of his future discontent were planted, and the time for harvesting that crop came with the interview we have seen.

THE SOLUTION

The solution to the problem of Charlie Bigshot is easy to write down and easy to agree with – and very difficult indeed to carry out. Before we hire anybody, before we even write out the advertisements for the job, or speak to the recruitment consultants, let us ask: where can this job lead to in, say, ten years' time? And don't let's say: 'Oh, that depends purely on the person himself; the job can lead anywhere.' That's just a cop-out. Perhaps we have to take a deep breath, grit our teeth and admit that it may be a dead-end job; that the successful applicant may find himself shunted into a backwater from where his chances of getting anywhere near the promotion ladder, much less climbing it, are non-existent.

You don't like the term 'dead-end job'? Nobody does. We reject the idea that we have the sort of department or section or division of a company where such things exist. But take a walk through your office or factory and look around you, and I promise you that you will find people in jobs who, *no matter how good they are*, will never rise above what they are doing now.

When you recognise this, don't be depressed and don't panic; it is as it should be. There will always be the dead-end jobs, and (and this is the point) there will always be the people who want that kind of job. In your organisation right now there are people who want to stay in precisely the positions they occupy at present. They have no thought of promotion and they would be shocked and horrified if you offered it to them. Wonderful! They are where they want to be, doing what they were hired to do.

But, when we realise that the vacancy we want to fill is either a true dead-ender, with no chance of promotion, or that at best it will mean that the successful applicant will be in that job for Xteen number of years, then let us examine the applicants very carefully indeed. Let us make it very clear to him/her what the job is now and what it will be in the future. It is better to chase away one potentially good person than to hire someone who wants the job merely as a quick stepping-stone to higher things, and the quicker the better.

Some managers on reading the above will shake their heads and smile confidently. 'There are no dead-end jobs in our company,' they affirm. 'We promote on merit and we promote across the board. Anybody in the organisation could become the Chief Executive Officer of this company – *anybody*.' Sure, and I could win the London–Brighton Marathon, so long as half of the runners lost their way and the other half lost their memories. It could happen, it just isn't very damned likely.

Hire the person for the job. Tell that person where the job can and cannot go. Don't fool people and, more importantly, don't fool yourself.

4

The timid supervisor

Suzy Mousey has worked for Paula Wolfe for three years. She can hardly be described as a dominant personality. In fact she blends in with the office furniture. However, she has always been a hard and competent worker with an excellent attitude. Nothing is too much trouble for her and she will go around looking for work when she has finished her own. For these reasons Paula gave her a small promotion recently, and Suzy now has two girls working for her.

Paula is beginning to regret the promotion since it seems that Suzy's little department is producing some headaches. Suzy's girls seem to spend a lot of time with their heads together, whispering and giggling and not doing much work. Suzy handles this by ignoring it for a time and then yelling at them, and these sessions often end in tears from Suzy and sudden visits to the rest-room.

Paula has opened the subject of Suzy's problems with her once or twice but she assures Paula that everything is fine. She clearly doesn't want to discuss the matter. The work is indeed being produced, but Paula suspects that Suzy is doing most of it herself, since she seems to take a heavy brief-case home most evenings.

After much sitting at her desk staring into space and breaking pencils, Paula has decided that whether Suzy wants to or not, she is going to have to discuss the problem. She believes that the best time for the talk will be after hours, so that no interruptions will be likely, and also so that the rest of the staff don't see a door-closed type of interview going on, which could start the office grapevine going. She has asked Suzy casually if she could stay after five o'clock, if Suzy is sure it won't clash with her plans. No plans, no clash, Suzy has assured her nervously. This doesn't mean much since Suzy's manner these days is chronically nervous. Paula has arranged for a tray with coffee to be in the office, and when Suzy knocks at the door she gets up to open it instead of yelling 'Come in!' as she usually does to anyone else.

Suzy at first refuses the offer of coffee, but Paula says: 'Oh, nonsense. I'm sure we both deserve a cup; it's been a long day.' Suzy sits on the edge of her chair, knees and feet together, chin down and eyes on her coffee cup.

Paula (tapping a bulky file of papers on her desk). Suzy, these Monthly Variable Costs Returns you submitted this morning–

Suzy (looking startled): What's the matter with them, Miss Wolfe?

Paula: There is nothing the matter with them; they are correct, as they always are, and you gave them to me on time as you always do. (Suzy looks relieved. Paula riffles through the file): Tell me, Suzy; who did them?

Suzy: Who did them?

Paula: Yes. Which of your girls did them – Sandra or Kim?

Suzy (hesitating): Why, I did them this time. The girls were busy with the forecasts for Mr Bailey.

Paula: You did them last time, too, didn't you?

Suzy (almost inaudible): I – may have. I can't sit doing nothing all day.

Paula: Well, you certainly don't do nothing, and that's what I want to talk to you about. Suzy, by my calculations you have done at least eight hours' work at home in the past three days, and that's all wrong. You are not supposed to have to take work home.

Suzy (miserable, eyes still fixed on her coffee cup): There's – there's more work this week than usual. I can't ask the girls to work overtime.

Paula: Let's talk about your girls. On Tuesday Kim was out of the office for nearly two hours. On Wednesday Sandra got to work forty minutes late. (Suzy is mute.) Well?

Suzy: Kim had a dentist appointment; I said she could go. Sandra's train was delayed.

Paula: Kim had a *hair* appointment – unless her dentist does highlights and blow-drying. Sandra comes in on the same line that I do, and there were no delays on Wednesday. (Suzy's face is red and her eyes are filling with tears.) I haven't been spying on you or your girls, Suzy. Those two instances happened to come to my notice one after the other. But doesn't it seem that you do have a problem?

33

Suzy: If – if you want me to resign, I'll understand–

Paula (suddenly irritated): Damn it, of course I don't want you to resign. Did you think that I asked you to stay behind so that I could fire you?

Suzy: Yes, I thought you might. I know I haven't been doing the job as well as you expected me to when you gave it to me. I thought perhaps I should resign to save you the embarrassment of firing me.

Paula: Then you are a bigger-(waves her hands about). Sorry, sorry, sorry. (Takes a deep breath.) Suzy, I do not have the slightest intention of firing you.

Suzy: Do you mean that, Miss Wolfe?

Paula: Of course I mean it. If you left I would be in a real jam.

Suzy (Tears gone): You *do* mean it.

Paula (Earnestly): When you were a clerk you had the best work record of anyone in the office. Why do you think I promoted you? So that you could show your girls how the job should be done. And that, Suzy, is the trouble. You are not showing them how to do the work, you are doing it yourself, and that is not what I promoted you for.

Suzy (with the first faint touch of spirit she has so far shown): Oh, that's not so, Miss Wolfe! Kim does all the work on the print-outs, just as I taught her, and Sandra is responsible for checking the Purchase-Receiving–

Paula: I know, I know. I didn't mean you literally and physically do every bit of the work. All the same, Kim and Sandra are doing nothing but the basic

34

routine stuff, and it does not take them a full working day. The rest is done on your desk or at your home, and you know that this is true.

Suzy: But – when I ask them to do more–

Paula: Yes? When you ask them to do more?

Suzy: They say they're too busy (suddenly she puts her face into her hands and bursts into tears).

Well, this interview has finally arrived at the moment of truth. Paula Wolfe has taken long enough to get to the real problem which is, of course, Suzy's management – or total lack of management – of her little work force. What do you think? Should Paula have been more direct? Should she have dispensed with the coffee-tray and after-hours informality, and come right out and socked Suzy with the clear fact that she had no control over her team? Perhaps in Suzy's already nervous state that sort of treatment would have put her into shock, so perhaps Paula has done as well as she could so far (apart from almost losing her cool for one brief moment, but she recovered from that with no tail-feathers lost).

So now she has her supervisor crying up a storm, broken, no defences left. Not a pleasant situation, and not one which Paula wanted. Where does she go from here?

Paula (Sits and waits. Eventually Suzy's sobs grow quieter and she gets herself under some sort of control. Paula opens a drawer and tosses a packet of tissues across the desk. She smiles at Suzy): There you are, blotting-paper for the emotions. I use them, too.

Suzy (snuffling into a wad of tissues): I d-don't believe you ever use them. At least, not for – not for–

Paula: Not for blubbing into? You have no idea of the times I have locked the door and had a good private cry. We girls are lucky. Men can't cry it all out. (Still friendly, but more businesslike) Now; what are we going to do about your problem? Say the word and I'll fire Sandra and Kim tomorrow. Shall I do that?

Suzy (horrified): No!

Paula: Why not?

Suzy: Because it's not their fault.

Paula: Whose fault is it, Suzy?

Suzy (with her eyes shut tight): It's my fault. It's my fault. There's nothing wrong with Kim and Sandra. They are good girls. It's just that – I'm not a supervisor! I don't know how to manage people! (The dam has burst now.) Oh, Miss Wolfe, I knew I shouldn't have agreed to take this promotion. I knew I wasn't right for the job, but you said I would get the hang of it in no time and I didn't want to disappoint you; and now – (the tears are starting again) now I *have* disappointed you!

Paula (hurriedly; she doesn't need another waterworks display): All right, Suzy; all right. Do understand that I am not blaming you. All this is not your fault. If it's anyone's fault then it's mine.

Suzy: Oh, no!

Paula: Oh, yes. When I threw you into the job without any real preparation or training, I simply didn't have my mind working properly. I haven't done anything to help you, either. Anyway, all that is in the past. From right now we are turning over a new page and starting clean. Here's what we do: first, I want you to put on paper all the duties and responsibilities of your section. Everything you and your team have to do, stick it down. Can you do that?

Suzy: Oh, Miss Wolfe. I already have that on paper. I wrote it all down when I took the job on.

Paula (looks at Suzy): Yes, I suppose you did. Good. Then the next thing is to divide it all into three sections; two big ones and one small one. Who are the two big sections for?

Suzy: I suppose, Kim and Sandra.

Paula: You suppose right. And who is the small section for?

Suzy (in a subdued voice): Me.

Paula: Right! Your job is to *manage* more and *do* less. Surely you see that, Suzy? You are a supervisor; it says so in your personal file. Your job is not to do the work, it is to supervise others while they do it, isn't that so?

Suzy (still subdued): Yes.

Paula: Now. The other thing that is going to happen, and I could kill myself for not doing it long ago, is that you are going on a course.

Suzy: A course?

Paula: A crash course in supervisory skills. I ought to be shot for giving you a job and not having you trained for it. (She fishes in a drawer and pulls out a brochure) Here's the syllabus: Leadership

Philosophy, Motivation, Personal relations, Time Control, Job organisation, Appraisal – the lot. This will give you the expertise you need. How does it sound?

Suzy: It sounds interesting.

Paula (Warmly and convincingly): Interesting! It's more than interesting, Suzy, it's the road to success for you. The course starts on Monday week and I'll put you on it tomorrow. In the meantime, remember; what has happened is not your fault. Let's forget the past and look ahead. There is no reason why you shouldn't do a terrific job once we have each person's job specifications set out, and once you have learnt how to be an effective supervisor. Right?

Suzy (convinced at last): Right, Miss Wolfe. Thank you.

Problem solved! Everything happened just as Paula Wolfe had outlined. The job specifications were set out, this time with the two clerks responsible for most of the work and Suzy responsible for supervising, checking the work for content and accuracy, and herself doing only some of the more critical and confidential work.

Ms Wolfe debated with herself the advisability of hauling Kim and Sandra into her office and stripping some hide off them for past misdemeanours and laying on the line what would happen if they didn't really get down to it under the new set of rules. She decided not to do this, realising that it would erode any last remaining shreds of authority which Suzy might have had. She confidently expected that after the supervisors' course Suzy would be in a much better position to handle the present situation or any which might arise in the future.

Pleased that she had handled a potentially explosive problem with diplomacy, despatch and a fine regard for the feelings of her staff and the requirements of her job, Paula Wolfe treated herself to a piece of Mexican silver jewellery and did a little mild swanking to her PIP (Presently Important Person).

HOW DID SHE DO?

How did Paula do? How did you like the way she handled the situation? Could she have done any better? The Suzys of this world can be particularly irritating creatures, and any prolonged contact with them produces an intense desire to take them by the shoulders and shake them until their teeth rattle, but while Paula comes across as a rather forceful and direct personality she managed to keep her hands off Suzy, and on the whole we might feel that she didn't do a bad job at all.

The truth is, of course, that Paula would have spent much more time than she did in order to save the situation – which meant saving Suzy – for the best reason in the world, which is simply that Suzy was Paula's choice for the job in the first place, and no way is Paula going to admit that she made a bad choice. She will fight tooth and nail to protect her decision; whatever it takes, that she will do.

Recognise this whenever you see a manager taking an action which does not jibe with the facts or with that manager's normal actions or personality. He may simply be protecting his investment in a decision which he made some time ago and which now threatens to blow up in his face. It's human, it's natural, and it happens all the time.

Every day I have to drive through a set of traffic lights which should never have been installed, because they produce a bottleneck and hold up traffic without in any way benefiting either the traffic or the pedestrians using that crossing. All this is obvious to everyone, but will the lights ever be removed? When the clown who ordered their installation reaches the age of 65 and retires with his gold watch they will come out the very next day – but not until then. Their removal now would be an admission that a mistake was made, and the clown in question would suffer the tortures of the damned before he allows that.

Not that we accuse Ms Wolfe of cynically protecting Suzy in order to cover up a bad decision; no doubt she honestly feels that her solutions will do the job.

WHAT HAPPENED?

Suzy went on the supervisors' course and came back with a fat manual, a bulging notebook and a vocabulary of buzz-words like 'job enrichment' and 'quality circles'. She sat down with Kim and Sandra and explained the new work apportionments. She happily assured her boss that everything would now be hunky-dory; no problems, no hassles.

It was a month or so later that complaints began to come in from other departments. Returns were late, figures were inaccurate, presentation was sub-standard. Sandra resigned. In her exit interview with Paula she was evasive and off-hand. She 'just wanted a change'. No, nothing wrong, nothing to do with the company or its managers, no complaints. No, didn't need a reference, thanks. G'bye, and good luck to you, too.

Suzy hired a replacement (they had covered 'Staff Selection' in the course) but things got no better; the work was simply not being done at the standard and in the time required. Paula broke a few more pencils and called Suzy in for an interview. This time there was no tray of coffee and the interview took place in the middle of the afternoon.

Paula: Suzy, what the hell is going on?

Suzy: Going on?

Paula: Come on, woman. You know why you are sitting here. I spend my time trying to make peace with half-a-dozen department heads every day because your section has fouled something up. What's happened?

Suzy: We – we are getting more of a work-load coming through these days, and my girls–

Paula: I have analysed the work over the past six months and if anything there is slightly less than there was. Come on, now, Suzy. Your girls are not turning the work out and when they do it isn't up to standard. The work is not difficult. Kim has shown that she can do it, and this new girl – what's her name?

Suzy: Darleen.

Paula: Good God. She came with good references; she's all right, isn't she?

Suzy: Oh, yes.

Paula: Well? (Suzy remains silent) Suzy, two months ago we had a talk. We decided on certain changes. We did the things we decided. You went on the course. We set out the job specs. We both thought that we had solved the problem and now the problem is worse than it was before. *What the hell is wrong?*

Suzy: I don't know, Miss Wolfe. I just don't know. (Crying) Oh, I'm so unhappy!

WHAT WENT WRONG?

Well, as Paula wanted to know, what the hell *is* wrong? Let us assume certain basics:

1. The work load on Suzy's section is not excessive.

2. The two clerks are sufficiently trained to be capable of doing the work.

3. Suzy was technically competent to handle the 'mechanical' part of the job – inspection, correction, and allotment of the work.

4. Working conditions, pay, amenities and so forth were satisfactory.

5. Paula Wolfe was technically competent at *her* job.

Assuming all this, what are we left with? We are left with Suzy herself. Not the mechanical, technical part of her – that we know she can do. It is the people part of Suzy which is wrong (It must be so, because there is nothing else). Suzy is simply not a manager of people. Her personality, her inter-personal relationships, her basic character are such that she will never satisfactorily be able to manage people, and this is something that many people in business are unable to accept – in Suzy's case and the case of many others, no amount of *training* will ever make her capable of handling people.

I run management training; it is part of what I do for a living. If Suzy had ever attended one of my clinics it would have been a waste of time and money. I have never turned a bad manager into a good manager, and I don't believe that anybody else ever has either. Training can only give a person the ammunition, that's all; he has to bring his own gun into the fight.

THE SOLUTION?

Fire Suzy.

Certainly, fire Suzy. Why not? Paula Wolfe has done everything she possibly can to help Suzy. She has had talks with her, she has helped her reorganise workloads, she has arranged for the best training – still Suzy is not producing the performance required of her and, worse, she now shows every sign of cracking up under the strain of doing a job for which she simply is not suited by temperament, inclination or talent. So, fire her!

But it isn't as simple as that, is it? Let us not forget that Suzy did not ask to be promoted. She was probably not even consulted as to the promotion. What's the betting that Paula Wolfe merely called her in one day and said: 'Good news, Suzy! Your hard work is being recognised. From next month you will be supervisor of your own section. You will have your own private office, a staff of two, and of course a big increase in salary. Isn't that wonderful?'

And Suzy must have said, in a daze: 'Yes, Miss Wolfe. That's wonderful!' She wasn't given any choice, she wasn't asked whether she wanted the job or not. Most important, she was not told: 'This is what the job is all about. These are the responsibilities, the limits of authority, the standards expected of you. *Do you think you can do this job?*'

There is a weird form of reasoning which takes place in the minds of people who have been thrust into a position of authority and responsibility. Perhaps this rationale went through your mind when you were first given a job where you gave out some of the orders instead of obeying them; I know it did in my mind. It goes like this: 'Goodness! Can I really do this job? All this is so new to me – suppose I'm not cut out for this responsibility? Oh, well; the big brass obviously think I can do it or they wouldn't have given me the job. Now, they are very smart people, so I suppose they know more about my abilities than I do.'

More – there may even be a thought, not articulated and not, perhaps, even acknowledged, that *they* gave me the job, I didn't ask for it, so if I fail it's *their* fault, not mine.

It is not difficult to avoid the catastrophe which has overtaken Suzy (it is a catastrophe; her career, everything she has built up in her time in the company is falling about her ears). All that is necessary is to evaluate two things – Ability and Motivation. Can he do the job, and does he want it. In Suzy's case we still don't know whether or not she wanted it in the first place – but we certainly know that she can't do it.

I could kill some of the executives who attend my management Clinics who nod in total agreement when

I warn against the theory that if someone is the best one in the workforce then it must follow that he is the obvious choice for promotion to a management job. They agree with me – no argument, the man is dead right. Then they go back to their jobs and promptly promote the best clerk, salesperson or artisan to be a sueprvisor over the other clerks, salespersons or artisans. We would think it madness to give a tuba to a violinist and expect him to play it. Yet we unhesitatingly pick the best violinist, make him the conductor, and expect him to pick up a baton and immediately lead the orchestra through Beethoven's Ninth as though he had been doing it all his life. Crazy.

Paula Wolfe knows very well that she can't fire Suzy. She knows that she blew it in the beginning by not evaluating Suzy's ability and motivation. But she also knows that she can't keep Suzy in the job. She is going to have to find a job in the company somewhere where Suzy can use the undoubted talents which she does possess – accuracy, the ability to get through a tremendous amount of work and to do it without supervision, a fine attitude towards the company. She is going to have to do this without it seeming as though Suzy is being demoted. The ideal job is one with a good deal of responsibility without the need to use any authority over others. She should be put in charge of *things* instead of *people*. In fact, according to the definition of a manager at the beginning of this book, she must be taken out of a managerial position, since a manager is someone who manages people, not things. All this, without in any way humiliating her.

That's your solution, Ms Wolfe – and when you are looking for a replacement for Suzy, evaluate her

Ability and her Motivation, and avoid the drama of The Timid Supervisor.

5

The *where* dictates the *how*

The citizens of Mombasa, sitting as they do practically on the equator with the sort of weather which goes with that position, don't paint the walls of their houses bright orange. If you start up a high-class restaurant you don't situate it overlooking a railway line.

The venue and its atmosphere dictates to an astonishing degree the tone of a meeting – any sort of meeting, although here we are concerned with meetings between managers and their people. I remember a job which I applied for where the first interview was in the office of the chief executive of the company; all mahogany, dark blue leather, panelling, and awards on the walls. The tone was dignified, remote, austere. For the second interview I was invited to the big man's house. His den was adorned with fishing trophies and he apologised for not having had time to change from his tennis gear. The interview was chatty, first-name, beer-drunk-from-the-can.

Now this is hardly surprising to you. We have all been affected by surroundings. Everyone is familiar with the effect which is deliberately created by the marble pillars of a financial institution or the silver and purple furnishings of a casino. What we sometimes forget is that the discussions we have with our people can be influenced tremendously by the venue and the surroundings generally. They can even be a contributing factor in the success or failure of the meeting.

What are the options? Where can you talk? Well, the answer is: almost anywhere. I remember thinking that a boss of mine had fallen out of his tree when he walked into my office in the middle of a busy morning and suggested that we go for a walk in the park. In the serenity of old oaks and the cheerfulness of new marigolds he gently pointed out where I was going wrong in my handling of a delicate situation in my work, and set my feet on the right path. We fed peanuts to the squirrels as he complimented me on the progress I had made in one aspect of my work, and watched goldfish in the lilypond as he put things in perspective for me. An unforgettable experience, and one where the venue set the tone and helped him to get things across in a way which would have been quite impossible in the master/servant atmosphere of his office.

Other possibilities, some obvious and some not so obvious:

YOUR OFFICE

The most common place, chosen for its convenience and for the fact that you are on your own ground there and everyone else is a visitor. Stay behind your desk and the tone is more formal. Come away from it and sit with your staff member in chairs placed around a coffee-table in another part of the room and it is much more friendly. This may or may not be a good thing. If your people become used to seeing you behind your desk for some interviews or around the coffee-table for others they will quickly catch on that the desk probably means trouble of some sort and the coffee-table means no sweat. People being what they are you can expect them to work out some pet names for the types of interview they can expect from you. If this doesn't bother you, if you like the idea that where you sit will quickly set the tone of the meeting, then go ahead.

HIS/HER OFFICE

Or, his area in the repair ship / her cubicle in the stock department / his desk in the computer room. By going onto the territory of your staff member you are paying him a visit, which may show any one of several things. You may be acknowledging that he is worthy of the trouble of going to see him. You may be showing that you realise that his time is valuable and you do not wish to drag him away from his work. You are recognising that this is his ground and that you are, as it were, a guest here.

In any event you are almost certainly indicating that the visit will not be to admonish, correct, vilify or threaten, since you would not do these things in public, and your worker's place of business is not likely to be especially private. It is a gracious act to 'visit' your people in their own little area, and managers should do it more often. It does the person's morale no harm at all to have it shown that the big chief thinks it worthwhile to come down out of his ivory tower and chew the fat with him; it is good both for the person concerned as well as for his colleagues.

NEUTRAL GROUND

My manager walking through the park with me was a classic case of choosing a De-Militarised Zone or neutral ground for talking with a subordinate. Neutral ground, which almost always means outside the office, factory or other work-place, has the obvious physical advantages of complete privacy and no interruptions whatever. ('I know you said no calls, sir, but this person says he simply has to speak to you'.) I seem to have been able to get closer to my team members in the quiet neutrality of an out-of-the-way restaurant or café, travelling in a car – either theirs or mine – or simply copying my old boss and going for a walk with the person. I learnt that this habit got to be called 'Beer's Walkie-Talkie', but it didn't seem to be applied in a derogatory sense so it didn't bother me.

YOUR HOME

Not to be done too often unless you have a very understanding and patient marriage (or whatever) partner who doesn't mind your turning your home into a branch office of the company. I know that a manager's home is often used for high-level, shirt-sleeve conferences, but I prefer, if for some reason the office is not considered suitable, to hire a hotel room for the occasion.

For a single-person discussion the fact that you have invited him into your home means that, at least for that crowded hour of glorious life, you are elevating him to the peerage, and there may be very good reason to do this.

HIS/HER HOME

Now why would you want to go to the homes of your people to discuss something with them? One reason only – to bring his/her partner into the act for some special reason. I haven't ever done it and I have knowledge of very few times that it has been done. One instance was related to me; it was where the manager was proposing to transfer a staff member to an overseas subsidiary of the company. This was obviously a big step, and the manager wanted to make very sure that the man's wife understood the implications of the proposed move and that she was completely behind her husband's decision to accept the transfer. Apparently in this case it worked very well. The wife said at the end of the visit that she had in fact been a little doubtful about the move, but now that she knew more about it she was all for it.

There can be very few occasions where such a visit is necessary, and it goes without saying that from the staff member's wife's point of view the manager is a visitor to her domain. He could even seem to be an interloper. The attitude could easily be: 'Well, he may be Charlie's boss, but he isn't mine, so he had better not put a foot wrong in *this* house.' Let's tread on eggs here.

So much for the possible venues for discussion, for the 'One-on-One' talks with your people. I don't wish to make too much of this section or give the impression that we should take the person rock-climbing or scuba-diving every time we wish to discuss anything with him. Most of the time the most obvious and best place is still the office. All that is necessary is to be aware that there are other places, and that to a surprisingly large extent these places set the tone of the meeting and can help significantly to move the discussion along the lines you wish. The *where* does indeed dictate the *how*.

6

The life of the party

Herbert Pally is the friendliest and most endearing character in Victor Black's sales group. He is on first name terms with everyone in the company; every clerk and typist has a smile for Herbert. He is the automatic choice for Father Christmas at the children's party and he can enliven the dullest sales meeting with imitations and conjuring tricks. He is involved in a score of outside interests from the PTA and Junior Chamber to fund-raising for several charities.

Herbert's sales are fair, although Victor would like to see them higher. His relations with his customers are excellent – he is 'Herbie Boy' to all of them. On a recent product knowledge test he came bottom of the group: 'Heck, boss, I don't need all that stuff – my customers buy from me because they like me. A salesman's first job is to sell himself.'

Victor knows that Herbert has a regular Wednesday afternoon golf match; he also knows that if he taxes Herbert with this he will say that he is playing with customers, and that this may well be true.

Is there a problem with Herbert Pally?

Herbert Pally has an appointment with his manager. There is nothing unusual about this meeting; it is the normal monthly appraisal which Victor Black does with all of his sales team. It is an informal thing and the results don't go into the salesman's personal file as do the results of the twice-yearly appraisal. Victor is looking at the print-out of the returns from Herbert's territory when Herbert walks in.

Herbert: Hiya, Vic! How's the boy?

Victor: I'm all right. Sit down.

Herbert: Now comes the day of judgement, does it not? The judgement can't be bad this month though. The computer print-out which adorns your desk has no doubt informed you that your favourite salesman, everyone's friend, Pally, Herbert, has made his quota on all five product ranges. Hooray for me!

Victor: I see it. I also see that you have only just made quota in each product range.

Herbert: Vic, the way I see it, quota is quota; if I've reached it then I've reached it.

Victor: Yes, but it's interesting, all the same. Herbert, I warn you, if I find that you have been holding back orders once you have made quota for the month I will chop you up and feed you to the vultures.

Herbert: Now, Vic! You hurt me when you say that. Would I do such a thing?

Victor: Would you?

Herbert: Cross my heart and wish to die, no.

54

Victor: Well, if I find you doing it you will get your wish. What the print-out does show is that your Collectibles are well below standard. A sale isn't a sale until it's paid for – you know that perfectly well. You have five customers going into sixty days and two heading for ninety days in arrears. What about it?

Herbert (stops smiling for the first time): Hell, Vic, you know how I feel about that. I spend months getting the customer's confidence. I get him to call me 'Herbie' – he likes me! Then I have to go there and dun him for money. What does that do for the customer-salesman relationships which I spend so much time building up?

Victor: Customer-salesman relationships don't help the cash-flow situation. It's no good getting cosy with your customers if they don't pay.

Herbert: Yes, but can't Finance write to them -

Victor: No.

Herbert: Or Orders could phone them -

Victor: No.

Herbert: Or -

Victor: No! Stop wriggling around. Collecting slow payers is the job of the salesman who made the sale in the first place. Now I am making a note of those seven customers and this time next month I want every one of them up-to-date. Clear?

Herbert: Clear. Hell, I came in here expecting to be told that I smell like Brut because my sales figures are right on the button, and suddenly I'm typhoid Mary because of a few lousy outstandings (Victor opens his mouth). Okay, Vic, okay. I'll dun my best customers for dough – which will make it a breeze when I have to sell them more product.

Victor (still looking at the print-out): Another thing. Where did you acquire a jet-plane and where did you learn to fly it?

Herbert: What? Vic, what are you smoking these days?

Victor: Well, you must be flying because you can't be seeing your customers by driving to them. Here's your call report for last month. On Tuesday the 18th you apparently covered – let's see – almost eight hundred miles and saw seven customers. Do you have any trouble finding places to land?

Herbert: Oh, that (he scratches his nose).

Victor: Yes, that. Now, you are not leaving this office until I get an explanation of how you can see one customer in Westville and one in Middleton on the same day without flying. You are ghosting calls, aren't you? You are just putting down any name you happen to think of, to try to fool me into thinking that you are doing a decent day's work, right?

Herbert: No! I wouldn't do that.

Victor: Then what the hell *are* you doing? (Has another look at the report.) Wait a minute – you actually took orders from both of these customers, and they are nearly eight hundred miles apart! (Light dawns. He sits back and looks at Herbert.) You phoned them. You sat on your arse somewhere and phoned them, and then you put them down on the report as calls. You bastard!

Herbert (defensively): Now wait a minute, Viccie -

Victor: Don't call me Viccie!

Herbert: Vic – Victor. Darn it, they *were* calls. I made contact with those customers and took orders from them. What does it matter whether I spent a lot of the company's money on petrol to go and see them, or some of my own – (he stops suddenly).

Victor(Slowly): Some of your *own* money. You sat at home and phoned your customers. What were you doing – baby-sitting while your wife went out shopping?

Herbert: No. It wasn't like that.

Victor: Can you give me one reason why I shouldn't fire you right now?

Herbert: You don't mean that!

Victor: Don't I mean it? You deliberately lie to me – don't interrupt me! You lie in a report. This is the first time I have spotted it, so Lord knows how long it has been going on. You know damned well that a 'call' on the call report is a physical visit, not a telephone call (He stabs the report with a finger). There is a separate column here for telephone calls, but you don't use that because then I would see just what a bloody loafer you are. You have a desk here with a telephone on it, but you don't use that; no, you make the calls at home so that I will think that you are rushing around the country in a hot and dusty car – (he stops, and his expression becomes even more furious). Hold everything. Hold every – bloody – thing. Let's have a look at your mileage returns for the month. (At this, Herbert looks really apprehensive. Victor runs his finger down the line of figures.) So. Now at last I understand. You are putting private mileage down as company mileage, riding for free on the company, and cheating on your reports. You are fired.

Herbert: No, Vic!

Victor: Yes, Vic! You are a liar and a cheat. I don't want you on my team, and when Mr Broome hears about this he won't want you in the company.

Herbert: (almost in tears): Vic – Victor. Please listen to me. I know it looks bad but I can explain -

Victor: You can explain nothing. Have you been putting down phone calls as physical visits?

Herbert: Yes, but -

Victor: Have you been putting down weekend mileage as business mileage?

Herbert: Yes, but -

Victor: Then you are out. Gone, finished, out!

WHAT DO YOU THINK?

Well! What started off as a routine appraisal ended on a note of high drama. Was Victor Black justified in summarily firing Herbert? Was that not a little drastic, considering that it was a first offence? Or was it the first detected offence, with the feeling in Victor's mind that he had been fooled for some time? Even so, wasn't it rather hard? Herbert always seems to have made his sales quotas, don't forget, and a person who does that

58

is doing exactly what the company wants him to do. How many people do exactly the job they are hired for?

There's no malice in Herbert, either; he gets on with the internal staff (which so many salesmen signally fail to do), he is a good team man, too. Would you stake him out on the ant-hill just for this transgression?

Ah, but his real sin was not doing the company out of a few gallons of petrol. Show me a person who has never fudged a little bit on his expense account and I'll show you a salesperson in his first week out on the road. No, the mortal sin – the unforgiveable one – was lying to his boss. 'Ghosting' calls, that is, saying that you have seen customers when you have not, is something which all sales managers view with a cold hatred. As one manager said to me: 'I can handle everything my people do wrong – everything they can possibly screw up – except lying to me. So long as they tell me the truth, no matter how bad it is, we can keep going. When they lie, I no longer know where I am.'

So we can understand Victor Black's reaction, arbitrary as it might have sounded.

WHAT HAPPENED?

In this particular company every person who leaves for whatever reason, goes through an exit interview. The interview is conducted by an official of the company who has nothing to do with the department of the person who is leaving. Herbert's interview is handled by Tom Bland, assistant personnel manager. It takes place in one of the interview rooms in the personnel department, the final week before Herbert leaves the company.

Tom: Mr Pally? I'm Tom Bland. It's Herbert, isn't it? Please call me Tom. Now, the purpose of this talk is to find out the circumstances of anyone's leaving the company. This does two things: first, it ensures that nobody has been unfairly dismissed, it allows people to have their say, freely and openly. Second, it sometimes shows up where we as a company are going wrong. If we see that a pattern is forming which shows a weakness in company policy then we can correct it. I have this form which I am going to ask you to help me fill in, but frankly, the form isn't as important as hearing from you in your own words exactly what happened.

Herbert (the chip showing large on his shoulder): What happened was that I got fired for a silly little thing, and Black didn't even let me explain!

Tom: Could you put me in the picture? I don't know anything of the details. I usually come into these things with no information at all. (He's a liar. He has Victor Black's full written report in a locked drawer of his desk.)

Herbert: I took a couple of good orders from two customers of mine, which put me well over my sales quota for the month, and I happened to put them down as 'calls' on my report. Well, to save time and money I had phoned them. There's no reason not to do that when you have as close a relationship with your customers as I have. Well, I did call them, but Black didn't agree, so he fired me. Just like that.

Tom: I see. But isn't there a separate listing for telephone calls on the monthly report? Seems to me I remember something like that. (He knows the monthly sales report by heart.)

Herbert: Look, I've been fired already. I don't need someone else calling me a liar all over again.

Tom: Good heavens, Herbert, I'm not calling you anything at all. It's my job to get things straight, that's all. Tell me, was that Victor Black's only reason for dismissing you? I haven't spoken to him yet (The 'yet' tells Herbert that he isn't going to get away with it, that he might as well come clean).

Herbert: Well, he made a big thing about mileage on the report (Tom says nothing). The – difference between private mileage and company mileage (Tom says nothing). Well, dammit, I saved the company a lot of money by telephoning those people instead of driving all the way to see them, so I -

Tom: Yes? So you -

Herbert (miserable and shame-faced): So I put down some private mileage as though it were company mileage.

Tom: And it was really that which made Victor Black decide to dismiss you?

Herbert: I – suppose so. Yes, it was that.

Tom: Do you think he was wrong? (Herbert remains silent.) What would you have done in his place? (Nothing from Herbert.) He trusted you, Herbert. Don't you think it was a shock to him to find that you would – mislead him like that?

Herbert (It bursts out of him): If I was Victor Black I would take more interest in my men! I would see that when someone has a baby he has a whole lot of expenses! I don't get the sort of money I should with my service record – the bloody company owes me a lot more than a few lousy gallons of petrol!

Tom (After a pause): And you felt that you were only taking what was due to you?

Herbert: Now wait a bit; you started off calling me a liar. Now I'm a thief as well? I didn't *take* anything! I used a bit of petrol, that's all. Is that a capital crime? (He stands) I'm sick of this. I don't have to take this. I'm going. (He walks out.)

WHAT DO YOU THINK?

Exit interviews are often painful and embarrassing things and no-one ever really looks forward to them. They can be very useful, though, which is why people persevere with them.

How do you think Tom Bland handled this interview? Could he have done anything which would have helped to end it on a more pleasant and positive note? It seems that Tom did as much as he could have. His job was to extract information and attitudes from Herbert, and this he did, with just the right amount of leading questions and the use of silence (such a valuable technique, this).

Tom Bland's own evaluation of his performance in the interview was that he had failed in one important aspect; no company likes to have any employee leave with, as it were, a bad taste in the mouth. Apart from obvious reasons for dismissal such as outright theft, deliberate disobeying of instructions and the flouting of authority, it is always preferable if possible to have a dismissed person saying to himself: 'I did wrong and they were justified in letting me go. At least, they did give me a fair crack of the whip; I was able to state my case.' Tom did not manage to inculcate this feeling into Herbert, but he may have been too hard on himself to call the interview a failure on these grounds. It is doubtful if anyone could have had Herbert feeling any differently from what he did. It was nothing that Tom did; it was in the end Herbert's knowledge that he was at fault which produced his attitude and which terminated the interview.

However, something interesting did come out of Herbert's outburst. He used the excuse of the high expense of starting a family, and this is surely worth following up. Was it merely an excuse, something thrown out as a red herring? Or is it worth while looking into the salary structure of the sales force? Staff remuneration has a way of sliding out of line unless we watch it regularly and continually. Are we forcing people like Herbert into a (to be dramatic) life of crime in order that they may pay their bills?

Tom Bland thought that a little research might be worth while, and he set up a small committee consisting of himself, Victor Black and the PRO of the company. After some hard work they came to the conclusion that while pay scales were satisfactory in the normal way there could be a case for helping out in some emergencies such as an addition to a family. They recommended to senior management that a 'Birthday Present' of, say, two weeks' salary should be handed out to a new father to help with the bottles and nappies. Management took up the suggestion and the little committee felt that it had achieved something.

Trouble is, of course, that by that time Herbert Pally was long gone. Would the extra cheque have stopped him from bending the truth in his monthly report? No, you're right, it wouldn't have. While he may indeed have found the expense of starting a family a little fierce *this was not the reason for his malefactions.* Consider the sort of person that Herbert was: friendly, people-oriented, his life full of outside interests, not sufficiently involved in his work to learn about the products he sells, and in general doing a less than perfect job. What is lacking here is any sign of killer instinct, of real *motivation* – and that is what the problem of Herbert Pally is all about.

A motivated salesman, one with a real sense of direction and with clearly-defined goals, does not sit on a telephone and call his customers instead of physically going to see them. Certainly, the telephone is a wonderfully useful sales aid, but it is not a substitute for a sales call and every salesperson, Herbert included, knows this. It is so easy for a salesman to get into the habit of thinking: 'My customers know me so well that I don't have to knock on their doors in order to see to them. Why waste their time? Let's ring them.' When he does this he is taking the first steps downhill in the selling business and it will not be long before he is on his way out.

So we see that Herbert's problem (and, therefore, Victor's too) has nothing to do with whether his car mileage is company or private. What we have here is a potentially valuable member of a team who has been allowed to drift into producing a half performance by doing a half job. How do you go about motivating a happy-go-lucky, slap-dash character like Herbert?

THREE WAYS TO STRAIGHTEN OUT HERBERT PALLY

1. *Scare the pants off him*

'Herbert, it is later than you think. You are thirty-two years old and you have just become a father. Let me assure you from personal experience that when you complain about the expense of having a baby you don't know what you are talking about. The expense hasn't even started. Clothes, schooling, the whole business of higher education – it starts now. And don't look at me for an increase in your salary because I can't give it to you, and do you know why? Because you are not earning what I am paying you now. If you are going to bring up a family you are going to need more money, and if you want more money you are going to have to earn it.

'Look at our team. How do you rate yourself in the six people we have? I rate you *fifth*. Everybody knows that we are going to promote someone to Key Accounts soon; who do you think it will be? If you were me, would you promote Herbert Pally? No, you would not. You still have a chance to make something of yourself in this company – past performances have been duly recognised – but the sands are running out and the time to start is now. Not tomorrow, Herbert, but today. It is later than you think.'

That is the classic way of motivating through fear, and don't think it doesn't work because in many, many cases it works very well indeed. It seems to work best with the lackadaisical type of person, the one who is drifting aimlessly through life, doing a bit here and a bit there, and making sure to smell the flowers along the way. It does not work where there is abundant willingness and limited ability; only the other way around.

2.   Point the way to the stars

'Herbert, listen to me. From today we are starting all over again. First, forget the mileage business on that report of yours. You are never going to do that again; private is private and company is company and never the twain shall meet, okay? Okay. The calls, too; from now on calls and telephone calls go into their proper places on the form. Forget all that, it's history. Now we draw a line and start again.

'Herbert, you have it in you to be a real success in this company. I mean it; maybe that's why I came down rather hard on you. I don't waste time picking specks out of rotten apples and if I seemed to lean on you it is because I know what you are capable of. You have important strengths. Have you thought what they are? Maybe it is time to examine them. Here's a piece of paper; let's write them down. First, you are a terrific people person; you can inspire confidence and trust in your customers. Second, you get on well with the office staff. The whole order department bends over backwards to help you by getting your stuff through on time. Next, you know your territory better than anyone else in the team knows theirs. Then again, you have a really sound knowledge of the way this company works, and that's something you get only from experience. You have a lot of things going for you, my friend!

'Now, to make sure that your good points are really working for you we have to straighten out one or two weak points. It would be a pity if we let them get in the way of your success. Now, what are they?

'First, product knowledge. You have a good brain and you might as well use it. Let's set up a programme – a timetable, if you like - and concentrate on boning up on each of the products in turn. You already have the broad facts about them or you would not have been able to sell them as well as you do. I want you to be able to answer any question you might get on any one of your products. Do you think you can do that in, say, the next six months? Great.

'Next, call frequency. Herbert, I have the feeling that you are letting small-talk turn into big talk. You know, we hear a lot about a salesman wasting a customer's time, but we don't hear much about a customer wasting a salesman's time – and it happens, doesn't it? Now, I know that you are a football buff. I bet you could tell me who won the cup for the last twenty years. The trouble is, your customers know this, too, and I have the feeling that too many of them like to rehash last week's game with you when you come around. Now a bit of this chatting does no harm and can even oil the wheels of good customer relations, but try to keep it to a reasonable level. I found when I was in the field that if I could get the *business* part of the call over first then I could have a bit of a natter about this and that afterwards, and extract myself from the call without too much time wasted.

'Herbert, let's concentrate on those two aspects for one month. I'll help you as much as you need; I'll give you all the time I can; but you are no novice and you can do most of it yourself. Then at the end of this month we'll see how it's going and set out a programme for next month.

'This is your chance to make something out of your

job in this company, Herbert, and as a new family man now is a great time to start. You are better than you think you are. Go ahead and prove it to yourself.'

That is the Motivation by encouragement method, and if you manage to push the right buttons it can work as no other way does. Every now and then you find that you have struck the precise chord and your person comes to life. A few times – too few – I have done something exactly right in motivating in this way and have watched in delighted disbelief as the person literally changes his life. It isn't often as dramatic as that, but by golly when it does happen it is worth the effort a thousand times over.

3. The Kick-Start

(This is delivered in an easy-going, relaxed manner; leg over the arm of the chair, coffee, cigarettes and no voices raised or indeed any sign that anything out of the ordinary is being discussed.)

'Herbert, you are a lazy slob. You know it, I know it, and what is more important, Mr Broome knows it. He makes unhappy noises whenever he looks at your returns. Now, he doesn't think that you are worth saving and I do, so you and I are going to prove him wrong. I'm not really doing this for you so much as for myself, because if you have to go I have the nuisance of having to hire and train a new person.

'Right; so I am going to save you if it kills you. There are three things wrong with you and my personal New Year's resolution is that in six months' time they won't exist any more.

'One: you are bone-lazy. Right – from this day forward you will appear in the office in person at seven-thirty before you go out into your territory. I shall be here to greet you personally. I know that this means that you will have to get up at sparrow-tweet, but you will get used to it. You may even enjoy it - the dawns are very pretty at this time of the year.

'Two: you don't know anything about your products. Herbert, shut up. This is not a two-way conversation, it is a list of non-negotiable instructions. You don't know anything about your products. Right. You will be in this office at eight o'clock each Saturday morning. Think of that: you can lie in bed for half-an-hour on Saturdays! You will be here promptly at eight and you will be ready to take a written test on one of your products. The product for this coming Saturday is Hellgrammite.

'Three: You don't make enough calls. Herbert, if you start explaining to me how big your territory is I shall stop being nice and patient and start being nasty and impatient. I know your territory better than you do and I tell you that you are not making enough calls. From now on I want a detailed planning sheet on my desk every Friday – yes, I know you do that already but from now on the sheet will not only have the customers' names, it will also have the approximate time that you will be calling on each one. Yes, you *can* do it, which is very lucky because you are *going* to do it. Now, it's always nice to get a suprise, and the surprise for you is that every now and then, probably when you least expect it, you will drive up to your customer's door and you will find me waiting for you, so you will have company for that call and for the rest of the day. Won't that be fun?

'Herbert, I am going to make a success of you in spite of yourself.'

The trick here is to be perfectly amiable; you are

not complaining or arguing, you are simply telling him what your assessment is of his failings and what you intend to do to get him on the right track again. As I say, it is relaxed, amiable and casual, but there is no doubt in Herbert's mind that every single word is meant and that if he does not toe the line the alternatives will be too awful to contemplate.

The whole point is that Herbert is worth saving. Indeed, if he can be straightened out he can be a very valuable part of the team. Think of it this way – if he was not on your team and he turned up tomorrow for a job interview, you would probably hire him, wouldn't you? When you consider some of the no-hopers who apply for jobs then he begins to look pretty good.

Whichever way you decide to handle Herbert – putting the fear of God into him, crying 'Excelsior!' and pointing the way up, or kick-starting him, the most important thing is to do it as soon as possible. He is at this moment in a comfortable groove, and he is rapidly wearing that groove into a rut. Catch him before the rut becomes too deep, and save him for himself and for you.

7

The prima donna

Hugo Fireball is David Barrett's top salesman. His sales figures are so far ahead of the rest of the team that it's positively embarrassing. He will drive a hundred miles through a snowstorm or a heatwave to close a sale and he doesn't know the meaning of the term 'Call reluctance'. He would barge into the houses of parliament if he thought there was the remotest chance of a sale. New business, old business, his territory or that of his team-mates – he will call and sell.

This is all very well, but Hugo has his weak points too. He usually misses sales meetings and when he does attend he is a disturbing influence. His call reports and other paperwork are either late or not forthcoming at all: 'Listen, mate; did you hire me to move product or to write you love-letters? Let those other guys fill in the forms while I do the selling.'

To him a customer is someone who buys big and buys often, and he will push very hard for a sale. David Barrett has already had one or two buyers who have phoned to say that they do not want Hugo on their premises again.

The managing director loves Hugo's sales figures and he has reminded David that it is very hard to get salesmen of the calibre of Hugo. The rest of the sales force doesn't like Hugo very much; this does not worry him one damn bit.

What would you do about Hugo Fireball?

David Barrett and Hugo Fireball are in Hugo's car. They are on their way back to the office after calling on an important customer where Hugo has taken a big order. David went along at Hugo's request 'To impress old Barnstaple at VTB Construction'. David feels that the only reason he was asked to come was so that Hugo could parade his selling skill before his boss.

Hugo (Loudly and off-key): 'My father was the keeper of the Eddystone lighthouse; he met a mermaid one fine day. The result of this was bastards three – two were fish and the other was me'. Hey, Dave, how about that Barnstaple character? Tells me that Worldwelders' Argon-arcs are as good as ours. Boy, did I straighten out his thinking!

David: Yes. There was a time when I thought he was going to straighten *you* out. You can't tell customers that their people are stupid.

Hugo: Ah, it all depends how you do it. The truth is that he *has* got some stupid welders in his shop. They don't deserve to work with the best equipment because they don't appreciate it. Hell, last month I took the torch out of the hands of one of the welders and ran a neater weld than he ever could. Showed the whole shop how to do it!

David: And made sure that the welder will have a hate against you and your company.

Hugo: He'll get over it. Barnstaple thought he wasn't going to give me an order today, did you notice? Thought he was going to brush me off. I showed him that Hugo Fireball never takes no for an answer.

David: Was it a good idea to high-pressure him like that?

Hugo: High-pressure? Dave, my lad, that wasn't high-pressure. Boy, when I high-pressure a customer he goes into intensive care. I just leaned on Barnstaple a little, that's all.

David: All the same, he did seem to have enough stock of the continuous rods. He won't nearly use it all by the next time you call.

Hugo: David, David, David. I was loading him with product, sure, and do you know why? Because tomorrow is the day the Worldwelder rep calls on VTB Construction, and what will old Barnstaple tell him? That Hugo the Great was here yesterday and we don't have storage space for any more welding rods, thank you very much.

David: Very well, so long as he doesn't get irritated with your loading him up every time you call.

Hugo: Relax, David. I know my customers and they know me. I know what I can do to them and for them, and they know what to expect from me. If you ever doubt this, walk out of your office and turn sharp left, and you will see a large sales chart on the wall, and whose name leads all the rest, like that guy in the poem? Hugo P. Fireball, the one and only, that's who!

David: I know, I know.

Hugo: Never fear when Hugo's near, old buddy. (Lifts his voice again in song) 'Caviar comes from the virgin sturgeon–'

David: Shut up for a moment. While we are on the subject of customers there's something I want to talk to you about. Your customer record cards are about three months behind, and Edith Pratley has been complaining–

Hugo: Don't worry; I'll fix it with old Edie.

David: It's not a question of 'fixing' it with anyone; those cards have got to be up-to-date. I've spoken to you several times about this, Hugo.

Hugo (Impatiently): Oh, for crying out loud, Dave. You aren't talking to one of the sheep in the team, you know. I am top dog in the company, and how do you think I got there? By doing a bloody good job, that's how. Those stupid record cards are for the new boys who don't know their customers the way I do mine. I tell you, I don't need to write that stuff down. I keep it up here in my skull and I *use* it; I don't put it on cards and stick it in a dusty filing system.

David: You are driving too fast.

Hugo: Don't worry. They never have a speed-trap on this road.

David: I don't give a damn about speed-traps; I tell you you are going too fast!

Hugo: Okay, boss; there – isn't that better?

David: Hugo, you know why those cards are kept. If

another salesman had to call on your customers how would he cope without that information?

Hugo: Now, why would I let any other salesman into my territory to screw up my customers?

David: Oh, for God's sake stop pretending that you don't know why we keep those records. A salesman could have an accident or be ill and off the road for several months. The territory has to be serviced. Or a salesman could leave–

Hugo: Don't worry, I'm not leaving–

David: Or be fired.

Hugo (Laughing): You aiming to fire me, Dave? Fire *me*? Now, that's a joke!

David: Now, just a minute! Who the hell do you think you are talking to?

Hugo: Hey, Dave, buddy! Relax, man. We are friends, right? Where did all this talk of leaving and firing come from?

David (After a pause): I want those record cards up-to-date.

Hugo: Sure. I'll see old Edie the first chance I get.

David: And another thing; I don't want you missing sales meetings. You have missed three Friday meetings in the last two months and it's not good enough.

Hugo: Oh, Dave, let's not go into all that again. Those damned meetings bore me to death (puts up a hand). Now, don't get mad. I'm not saying anything against your meetings, but they are for the sheep, Dave baby, not for me. All the little lambs on the team going baa-baa to each other while you teach them how to smile at the customer, keep their fingernails clean, don't waste the customer's time – come *on*, Dave; do you really think I need that? Please!

David: You needn't sneer at sales training, and don't keep calling your colleagues 'sheep'; they can't all be as marvellous as you. And anyway, the meetings are not all about sales training. We have product quiz sessions, last time we had a very good film on selling against low-priced competition – all right, perhaps you didn't need it, but we talk about lots of different things, and you should be there. What do you think it looks like when the team asks where you are and I have to pretend I didn't hear the question? What do you think it does to my authority? (He is making himself more angry.) Damn it, you will be at next Friday's meeting, do you hear?

Hugo: Okay, okay. Keep your hair on.

David: And when you are there I want to see a better attitude. The last time you condescended to attend a meeting you sat with your chair propped up against the wall and cracked peanuts the whole time. I want you present, on time, wearing a tie this time, and I want your participation in the discussions. The subject for this Friday is the problems of welding aluminium extrusions. You know something about that, so–

Hugo: Heck, I know everything about that.

David: Well then, let's have some contribution.

Hugo: You bet, Dave baby. (Loudly and off-key)

'There ain't many virgins among the sturgeons, that's why caviar is my dish.'

WHAT IS THE PROBLEM HERE?

The problem of Hugo Fireball is interesting because it is essentially simple. Not easy, heaven knows, in fact it is difficult, thorny, and fraught with perils; but there is nothing particularly complicated about it. Once we have cleared away the undergrowth we come to the single problem, which is this: do we go along with Hugo's nonsense for the sake of those lovely sales figures, or do we stamp on him just as we would any other team member the moment he puts a foot out of line?

Oh, surely it isn't a straight black/white, go/no-go alternative like that? Surely there is a middle ground we can find which will keep him producing at his present high level but at the same time get him to toe the line?

Before we examine the options let us look at David Barrett. How do you think he measures up to the requirements of his job based on what we have seen so far?

HOW DID IT GO?

David decided to have his talk with Hugo on neutral ground, and it is true than when a manager and his salesman are chatting in a car going to or coming from customers it can be a very good time and place. The two are both relaxed, sitting at ease while the scenery goes past. One interesting aspect of talking in a car is that the two people are not looking at each other, they are looking ahead through the windscreen. This can to a large extent remove the feeling of confrontation which can be present when facing each other over a desk in an office.

Whether or not this was a good idea in this case was debatable. Perhaps Hugo would have been in a less swaggering mood in his manager's office. As it was, David was in *Hugo's* car, which for a salesman means to a great degree his office, so David was the visitor on Hugo's ground. Perhaps it was not neutral ground after all.

In any event the main problem in the entire discussion was one of *command*. David as the manager lost command of the interchange at an early stage and never regained it, until towards the end. What should have been instructions came out as querulous and petulant complaints. Not to put too fine a point on it, David Barrett blew it from start to finish.

Why?

Well, in any duel the odds must favour the side with the greater firepower. Napoleon said: 'God is on the side of the big battalions'. In boxing the saying is that a good big man is better than a good small man. If David and Goliath were to have a rematch those in the know would still put their money on Goliath.

Hugo had the greater firepower in that duel – and it was a duel, of course. We can point out many weaknesses in the way that David Barrett handled the talk but his real problem was one of lesser firepower; he was simply out-gunned.

Again, why? Because of *need*. David needed Hugo more than Hugo needed David, and that's the answer right there. In most manager/worker meetings the manager has the greater firepower, simply because of his job. He has the authority, the clout, which comes from his ability to hire and fire, to affect the destinies of his people, and in all meetings between them this authority sits in. There it is – invisible, tacit, understood by both sides, and it colours and affects everything which is said and done in that meeting.

But not in this case. Hugo knows how good he is. All good salespeople know exactly and precisely how good they are. They know their worth to their company, and in the case of the real stars that worth can be considerable, even awesome; it can be – and here we have arrived at David's real problem – it can be more than the worth to the company of the person who is directly above them in rank. Hugo could be worth more to the company than David is.

So, David needs Hugo, and the sales of the department will be badly affected if Hugo should ever leave. Hugo does not need David; at least, not nearly as much. The real star can always put on his jacket, walk across the road, and fall into another job.

We can therefore sympathise with David Barrett. His dilemma has two horns: first he needs to keep the authority vested in his job as intact as possible, and it does look as if this means that Hugo has to be disciplined much more than is happening now. At the same time, David's chief gets a lovely rosy glow whenever he looks at Hugo's sales figures, and if ever they stopped coming he would look with extreme disfavour at the cause of the stoppage.

WHAT ARE THE OPTIONS?

There are three, and as we hoped, there *is* a grey as well as a black and a white; a sort of middle ground does exist.

1. *Unconditional surrender*

'All right, Hugo, you win. I admit that I don't want to lose you, that you are worth any three of the other salesmen, and I know I can't apply the same rules to you as I do to the rest of the team. Give Edith your rough notes and she will transcribe them on to the record cards. I'll give her a half-day off every now and then to make up for the extra work. Let me know when you are going to be in the office and I'll try to be there at the same time. You can tell me what's interesting in your territory, and anything that needs doing I will arrange to be done. Forget the sales meetings – except that you might like to be at the quarterly conference so that you can receive the top salesman award.

'That's it, then. Anything you want, just let me know. Where are you working tomorrow? You are taking two days off for some fishing? Well, good luck with your catch.'

How do you like it? You don't like it. It stinks. The moment you allow any single person on your team to get his thumb in your eye, you have lost more than the duel or the battle; you have lost the war. Any manager who took this first option as being the easiest way out of a troublesome situation would find himself in a position from which there is no relief, no recovery. One could say that in this special case it would be worth it to save Hugo for the company and, since management is the art of the possible, you do what you have to do, and the hell with what the purists and theorists say behind their ivy-covered walls.

All very well, but then the problem becomes not a problem of one person but of many persons. I should like to tattoo two words across the chest of every manager. The words would be in reverse so that they could read them in the mirror while they shave or put on their bras – whatever. The words are GROUP MORALE, and the word GROUP would be heavily high-lighted.

When it comes to fairness in their treatment, people are not stupid. The most imperceptive person quickly picks up on his antenna the least sign of discrimination against him. What about the rest of the team, when you start pressing Hugo's pants and cleaning his car and carrying his briefcase? How will they feel? How will they react? They will immediately know it when they have to walk the line and Hugo is allowed to dance to his own tune. What will happen to the morale of the group?

I once mentioned to a manager how heartily I condemned the practice of 'playing favourites' in a working group. He astonished me when he said: 'Oh, I play favourites. I have a team of eight salespeople and I get half my sales figures from two of them and the other half from the other six. You bet I play favourites! Those two get new cars and they pass their old cars down to the others. They get long weekends off while the other six have to work right up to Friday night. They get unlimited private mileage on their vacations. Oh, they have a good life; I see to that.'

I said: 'What about the other six? What do you do when they complain about the discrimination?'

He said: 'That's easy. I say to them, give me the same sales results and you get the same treatment.'

As it happens he was apparently a very successful manager, but that sort of management philosophy scares me silly. It is not only the Fireballs you have to keep happy, it is the whole team. If we had no star in the team we should not have the problem. Nor, of course, would we have the terrific performance. If on the other hand we had a whole team composed of Hugo Fireballs we would also have no problem; we would merely rush around after them, buying their theatre tickets, visiting their aunts and carrying their golf bags – while they made us rich.

The trouble is that we don't have no Fireballs in the team and we don't have all Fireballs; we have *one*, and that's the stone in the muffin you chip your tooth on. You need him but you also need the rest of the team. They may not be the greatest salespeople in the world but they are out there, seeing the customers and bringing in the business, and you can't do without them. They must have a good measure of group morale in order to function above the level of mere zombies, and the slightest little thing can destroy that morale. With this morale we have a *team*. Not perfect, heaven knows, but a team which can work – and play – together. Without it we have a bunch of individuals with no glue holding them together, no feeling for the unit or the company, no reason to exert themselves.

I say that nothing holds them together, but this may not be true. Even worse than a bunch of individuals could be a gang of conspirators, the traitors within your gates, who get together in dark corners and recount to each other the injustices which you and the company have perpetrated. Think it can't happen? It can happen only too easily. When it happens then you do have a team spirit, but it is hardly the spirit you had in mind.

No, unconditional surrender is out as a solution. No matter what benefits it gives you in the short term, over the long haul it can lead only to disaster.

2. *Lower the boom on him*

'Hugo, I have had it with you. I am sick and tired of you acting as though you are above the law. From now on you are just one of the team and you will conform. You have a job specification sheet; if you have managed to lose it, get another one from the stock room. Read it over very carefully and obey every single instruction on it. First transgression gets a warning, second one and you are on the carpet in the front office, third one and you are history. Get it? I hope you do because this is the only time I am telling you. That's all.'

Well! You certainly told Hugo, didn't you? That's the end of this nonsense of believing that he can act · like the crown prince around here. It will also show the rest of the team that we don't play favourites, that there is one law for all, no exceptions. Should be a big help to group morale.

Were I a betting man I would give, oh, say five to two that Hugo would hear us out, tell us exactly where to dispose of the job, and walk out. Should he stay then we have what every manager wants – a crackerjack salesman who conforms in every way to the policies and regulations of the company. Unfortunately those people are as rare as sugar-coated diet pills.

No, the odds are that we have lost Hugo, and we now have the delightful job of explaining to our boss that we have today taken a bold and decisive management step which will result in our sales volume dropping by twenty per cent.

Well, Unconditional Surrender and Lowering the Boom are the black and white options. What is the grey alternative?

3. *Appeal to his better nature*

'Hugo, I need to talk to you. I know that some of the rules we have for salespeople may seem petty and unnecessary for someone of your ability and experience. The trouble is that most of the group – and you know the standard of people that I have on the team – most of them have to be controlled in this way. Now, my job is hard enough as it is. When those guys see that you don't do the things which they have to do and when they see that I don't slap you down for not doing them, as I would slap them down, how do you think they feel? I lose all authority in their eyes, and when I try to enforce the rules I get mumbles and grumbles and general headwind.

'Now hell, Hugo; I know it's a nuisance, but how about coming to the meetings, and also keeping your records straight and oh, yes - washing your car. I give one of the men hell for a dirty car and yours is standing right next to it and it's even worse! Look; get it washed and put it on your expense account as entertainment; I'll pass it.

'Hugo, I'm not asking for much. You got three days off last month to watch the tennis championships, so what about a little give and take?'

That's the grey. How do you like it? It could work, too. Hugo Fireball might very well laugh, clap you on the back and say: 'Okay, David. For you, anything, old buddy. Don't worry, I'll do it.'

Problem solved?

Problem not solved. Problem enhanced, intensified, exacerbated, aggravated. What we have done here is carefully load a gun, give it to Hugo, curl his finger around the trigger while we hold the muzzle to our head. Hugo will do the things we have asked him to do, but he will do them as a special favour to us, not because they are the things which he has to do as a part of his job. Also, he will continue to do them only as long as they do not unduly interfere with his other activities, and there will always be the implicit threat that if *you* step out of line then *he* will apply the screw.

So *he* is now the manager. He dictates what he will or will not do. He calls the shots. You dance to his tune. Now you *really* have a problem, and it is one from which I cannot for the life of me see a way out. Can you?

Need it be said that no single person must ever be allowed to get into a position where he can blackmail the company? It is a truism to say that no-one is indispensable, but the real truth is that no-one must be allowed to *become* indispensable. I know that it is easy to read this, sitting back with no real problems bothering you and to agree that, yes, we mustn't let anyone get into that position. The problem is that people do get into that position. They get there by being good at their jobs, and what are we going to do to stop them? We can't say: 'Wait a minute; Paul or Paula is getting too good. It won't be long before he or she is able to dictate to us. We have to put a stop to this right now.' We can't say that. All we can do is recognise their worth and be grateful for it, but stamp on any indication that they intend to use this worth as a pistol to the head.

85

None of which means that a manager does not evaluate the worth of his worker, and when it comes to a decision about that person that he does not put that worth in the scale and give it full weight. You will always be prepared to bend over backwards for your really good people. Heavens, you have bent the rules for them many times, haven't you? Certainly you have. But the point is that this special handling is *your* decision, not forced by any threat, implicit or explicit, from your Hugo Fireball.

So. We have tried the three options: Unconditional Surrender, Lowering the Boom, and Appealing to his Better Nature. We don't very much like any of them. The first effectively strips us of all authority, the third puts a terrible weapon in his hand, and the second probably means that we shall lose him.

'I'm sorry,' says the harassed manager, having digested our thoughts on this case. 'Your theories may be fine on paper or in the conference room but I have a department, factory or office to run, and the truth is that I simply can't do without Joseph/Josephine. I have a foreman in the plant, a systems analyst in the computer room, a salesman in the field or a secretary in the office and without him/her I wouldn't know which way to turn. I have to keep that person and I will do whatever it takes to do so, so you can stuff your theories and options up the chimney and just let me get on with the job.'

Fair comment. It's so easy when you are not personally involved. All right, here's another case; it happened exactly as it is set out here.

THE FOOTLOOSE FOREMAN

Tony Burton, Plant Engineer of Western Textiles, was sitting in his office one day happily looking over the latest production figures – happily, because things were really going smoothly. Cost per unit, waste percentages, overtime; all were well within limits. As far as Tony was concerned the birds were singing and there was no single cloud in the bright blue sky.

Then a cloud knocked on his door. It didn't look like a cloud, it looked like Jim Teedle, his senior production foreman.

Tony: Come in, Jim, come in. Is that compressor on line three acting up again?

Jim: No, Mr Burton. It looks as though all it needed was a new gasket.

Tony: Fine. What can I do for you?

Jim (A trifle nervously): Mr Burton, I have had a letter, and in all fairness I thought I'd better show it to you.

Tony: What sort of a letter?

Jim (Handing over a piece of paper): Here it is.

Tony (Takes the letter. It is addressed to Jim and is from the Plant Director of Magnatex, the biggest opposition to Western Textiles. The part which jumps off the page and hits Tony between the eyes says: '–and we therefore confirm that we hereby offer you the position of senior Plant Foreman at our Mountville facility at a basic salary of–' The salary is eighteen per cent more than Jim is getting at Western. Tony puts the letter down slowly and carefully on his desk): When did you get this, Jim?

Jim: Er – yesterday, Mr Burton.

Tony: And you thought that I should see it.

Jim: Yes. In fairness to you.

Tony: Right; in fairness to me.

WHAT DO YOU DO NOW?

We can assume that Jim Teedle is a valuable man; if he is not then Tony Burton has no problem. He simply smiles, shakes Jim's hand, wishes him luck and speeds him on his way, at the same time reflecting that Magnatex must have a shaky staff recruitment system if they think that Teedle is worth that sort of money. If he is smart he might decide to get together with the personnel manager and check if salaries and wages in the plant have not fallen behind the going rate for the industry, but apart from promoting one of the plant foremen to Jim's job, Tony's life could go on pretty much the same as before.

But suppose that Jim Teedle is a really good man; sound, competent, and – and here's the point – very experienced in the complexities of Western Textile's plant procedure. Tony Burton can't go out and buy that experience; it has to be gained over years of on-the-job training. Tony doesn't want to lose that experience, and if Jim left, the experience would leave with him, in his head.

OPTIONS?

1. *Pay up and smile*

'Jim, this letter is quite a shock to me. I appreciate your bringing it in as soon as you got it. Frankly, I don't want to lose you, and although the money that Magnatex is offering you is above our ceiling for your job category, I'm going to see Mr Boulge right away and get him to meet the figure you have been offered. Can I come back to you this afternoon?'

If you need him then you are going to have to pay him what he could get elsewhere, not so? Let's see what Tony Burton thinks about our solution:

'Not a chance. I give him the money and in thirty minutes it's all over the shop that all you have to do is threaten to go to the opposition and Burton folds up like a sick caterpillar and hands over the cash. I simply can't afford to have that reputation.' Makes sense; scratch that idea.

2. *Kiss him goodbye*

'Well, Jim, this is a setback for the plant and bad news for me personally, but we can't possibly pay you the sort of money that Magnatex is offering you, so we won't stand in your way. If you are determined to take up the offer then I can only wish you the best of luck in your new job.'

Tony Burton could go this route and there is no doubt that it is the one which many managers would choose. It is surrender, of course, just as option 1 was surrender; the only difference is that option 1 was surrender to a person and option 2 was surrender to circumstances. It has little to recommend it except that at least we did let him leave without any bloodshed. As for that hackneyed phrase 'We won't stand in your way', it always irritates me. How can we 'stand in the way' of someone who intends to leave the company? Telephone his new manager and warn him that Jim is a streaker, a flasher and a general all-round trouble-maker? Chain him to the wall in the man's rest room? It's one of those pieces of flannel that people seem compelled to produce at times like this.

What does Tony Burton think of option 2?

'No. He's a good man and I won't just step aside and let him walk out of here.' Which leaves us with option 3.

3. *Talk it out*

Tony: Jim, sit down. First, thank you for coming to me with this letter. You and I have always been able to talk to each other and I value that relationship. Now, I am not going to try to talk you out of leaving Western, but what do you feel about this offer?

Jim (More relaxed than when he came in): Well, Mr Burton, it's a very good offer and, well, you know, what with the prices of everything going up all the time, I must say, well, it seems to me, I mean, it's a very good offer, and – (There is no way that Jim is ever going to be able to finish that sentence. Tony decides to finish it for him).

Tony: –And you feel that you should take it. Is that it?

Jim(Gratefully): Yes. I talked it over with Stella and

she is all for it. She was saying only last week that with little Jimmie going to school next year our expenses will be going up.

Tony: Well, that's understandable. Of course, in three months you will be due for your annual increase from Western. I can't say at this moment how much it will be–

Jim (With some spirit): It won't be as much as Magnatex are willing to give me though, will it?

Tony: No. However, while income is important to all of us, it isn't the only consideration, is it?

Jim (not believing this line): Isn't it?

Tony: Surely not. For instance, the working conditions in Western are recognised to be the best in the business. You are happy with your job here, aren't you?

Jim: Well, sure, Mr Burton; it's a good shop.

Tony: Of course it is! Then again, don't forget the perks.

Jim: Perks?

Tony: Perks (He starts putting down points on a pad). First, leave benefits. Next year you start the eight-year plan, and that's seven days a year extra leave (Jim nods his head slowly). Then, let's look at the pension plan. I don't know if you realise just what a terrific deal you have going for you on our plan. Also don't forget just how much you have built up in equity in the past eight years. It will make a big difference when you come to retire, and moving to another plan means that you lose all the part that the company has put in. This is already many thousands. Next point–'

And Tony keeps it up, adding up the strong points into a good case for Jim to stay just where he is.

This would be the option chosen by many good managers. It is not surrender because we are not considering meeting the offer of the other company; nor is it the cop-out of throwing our hands up and saying: 'All right, if that's the way you feel then go.'

We have written option 3 as though Tony Burton was actually speaking the part, but what does he really think about it?

'No. I'm not going to try to sell him on staying. I don't say it's the wrong way to do it but it isn't my way.' Well, you are a hard man to please; you reject all the options we have so carefully set out for you to use. All right, Mr Burton; what would you do?

HERE'S WHAT HAPPENED

What Tony Burton did do, and don't forget that this is a case history – it really happened – was this:

Tony (Hands back the letter to Jim. Calmly and clearly): You have one hour to come back in here and tell me that you have torn up that letter. That's all.

Wow! How did fine, gentlemanly Tony Burton suddenly turn into Ghengis Khan? That's not nice, to treat a person who has had the decency to come out into the open instead of going ahead behind his boss's back. Serve Burton right if Jim walked right across the road and joined the opposition without another word.

How could Tony Burton justify his action? I asked him and this is what he said:

'In the first place, no company writes a letter like that out of a clear sky. You don't put a job offer on paper, with all the details about salary scales, job responsibilities and future prospects without first having had an interview – perhaps several interviews – with the prospective employee. So, Jim Teedle had been playing footsie with Magnatex for some time before he came in and showed me the letter 'in fairness to me'.

'Second, he didn't walk into my office and tell me he was leaving. He didn't *resign* and then show me the letter; he showed me the letter and then just sat there. So he didn't do it 'in fairness to me'; the letter was his way of saying: 'If you want to keep me you are going to have to meet this offer. Even if you do meet it and I stay with you for now, don't ever forget that I can always get a good job elsewhere.' Now can you see why I didn't like any of your options? I had to remind him that he wasn't in charge of that interview, I was.'

All right, perhaps Tony Burton has a point there. But nobody can blame Jim Teedle for trying to better himself, and when he had the Magnatex letter in his hand, didn't it make sense to use it to try to improve his situation in his present job? Tony Burton again:

'Sure; Jim wasn't doing anything immoral or underhand by showing me the letter. But remember that he was asking for a big bump up in salary, and I couldn't have given him that even if I had wanted to. Then you have to realise that I know that our salary levels are among the best in the industry; they are much more than fair. So Magnatex was trying to buy Jim at an artificially high figure, and that seldom works out to the employee's advantage in the long term. The company gets the man they want, but by golly they are paying top money for him, and from him they therefore expect a superhuman performance, every day of his working life. Also it screws up their salary structure, so often what happens is that the new man simply gets smaller increases, or none at all, until his salary is in line with the other people - and just about what it would have been had he stayed with his old company.'

Oh, come on, Tony; don't pretend that you were so rough with Jim just to protect him from a horrible fate with the new company?

'No way! I am a manager, not Good King Wenceslas. All the same, if I needed justification for what I said to Jim, and I didn't, there it is right there. I know those Magnatex guys and that is the way they operate. Still, I am not Teedle's nanny, and if he had decided to join them I wouldn't have raised a finger to stop him.'

Tony Burton said: 'If he had decided to join them.' Does that mean that Jim Teedle didn't leave Western Textiles? What did happen after Tony had sent Jim out of his office with an ultimatum and a time limit? Let's ask Tony:

'Oh, he came back in twenty minutes and said: 'Mr Burton, I have torn up the letter.'

What was Burton's reaction to that?

'I didn't make a big thing of it. I said: "Good for you, Jim; I'm glad you have decided to stay with us and I think you are, too. By the way, I see that you have managed to reduce wastage on the milling machines by forty-two per cent; that's good housekeeping.'

A final question, Tony: if Jim had decided to leave would it have inconvenienced you?

'*Inconvenienced* me? My suffering aunt! I wouldn't

have known which way to turn. I would have been in *real* trouble. Don't even talk about it!'

POST MORTEM

So, it appears that when it comes to high-stakes gambling, Tony Burton makes Nick the Greek look like an amateur. By sending Jim Teedle away and telling him to tear up the offer from the opposition without allowing even one word of discussion on the subject, Tony was throwing everything into the pot – a winner-take-all game on one throw of the dice. Well, it worked. I saw Burton a year or so after this drama (remember, this actually happened) and I reminded him that the last time we talked he had just had his run-in with Jim Teedle. I asked him how Teedle was doing.

'Very well,' he said. 'Does a fine job and', with a cynical smile, 'A very good company man. Very *loyal*.'

As they say, don't knock it if it works, and Burton's strategy worked. He kept a man who was vitally important to the business and at the same time he demonstrated that he could not be blackmailed.

It worked, but most of us would still, I think, go with option 3. We would sit down with our employee and talk it over. After all, even Burton conceded that there was nothing wrong with Jim Teedle's talking to another company about a new position. It is something that all of us have done at some time. We would sit down and discuss the employee's present job conditions and the prospects for the future, and ask him to compare this very carefully with what he is considering taking on in the new company.

I see this as the duty of a good manager. It is not

a question of talking him into staying with us, perhaps against his better judgement, because that would merely postpone the evil day and, probably, give the employee a chronic grudge against us for causing him to lose out on a good job offer. No, we don't talk him into or out of anything at all; we make him look at both sides of the picture before he takes an important step in his career.

One of the few really good things I have done as a manager of people is to sit down with members of my staff in this way when they have been considering a change such as the one we have been examining. I recall with pleasure that some of them came back to me years later to say that they were grateful to me for helping them make the right decision. Once or twice it has happened that the best thing for them would be to take the offer, which of course meant leaving the company and me, and in these few cases I have simply shaken their hands (or kissed them, depending) and sped them on their way. There was nothing altruistic about that, it was pure business. If it is in the best interests of an employee to stay with you then it is your duty to point this out. If it is in his best interest to leave then I don't want him to stay, because his attitude and performance from that time on will be poison to the rest of the team.

We seem to have come a long way from Hugo Fireball, but the theme in both cases, Hugo's and Jim Teedle's, is similar. In both cases you have key people who could be in a position to blackmail you – it is not too strong a word – and in neither case could it be allowed to happen. It must never be allowed to happen, and if in the process of preventing it from happening you lose a good person then you bite on the bullet and find another good one to replace him.

I said about Hugo Fireball that the problem was essentially simple. Not easy, but simple – and that is about as simple as you can get.

8

Is there no such thing as *loyalty* any more?

'Loyalty: Having or showing continuing allegiance.'

Terry Prince is your best man. You hired him yourself six years ago, you trained him and supervised him, and you have taken some pride in watching him develop from a complete novice into a mature and highly competent key man in your team. Your boss always nods with approval when he goes over the appraisals with you and looks at Terry's form. You know that it won't be long before you are promoted, and when that happens Terry is the obvious choice as your successor.

Then one morning Terry taps at your office door.

You: Come in, Terry; since when have you had to knock and wait for permission to come into this office?

Terry: Do you have a moment, Peter?

You: For you? Always. Park your carcass. Coffee?

Terry: No, thanks. Peter, there's no easy way to say

this, but I have been offered another job and I'm taking it.

You: You're not serious.

Terry: I'm afraid I am. I'll stay long enough to help train a new man, but I'd like to leave before–

You: Wait a minute, *wait* a minute, damn it! Terry, what the *hell* are you talking about? You can't be telling me that you are walking out on me.

Terry: Sorry, Peter. Not that it makes any difference, but as it happens, I didn't go out looking for the job. Tangent Industries approached me and I agreed to talk to them. Well, the job is so attractive that I had to say yes.

You: But – but you throw this at me out of the blue–

Terry: Peter, I decided definitely only last night. Carrie and I discussed it until after midnight, and you are the first and only person I have talked to about it.

You: Why? Terry, Why?

Terry: Peter, it isn't just one thing, it's a whole lot of things. It's not that the immediate salary is so much better, for instance; it's the whole deal. This isn't a snap decision, Peter. I really feel that my future is with Tangent.

You (You are calmer, now): Is there anything I can say or do to make you change your mind? Are you absolutely sure that you are going to take this step?

Terry: I'm sure.

Exit Terry, and as he walks out of the office the chances are that you will throw your hands up and say something like: 'Is there no such thing as *loyalty* any more?'

Now, that is a reasonable reaction, isn't it? Terry Prince was your protegé. You took him into the fold and made him what he is today. Now it looks as though all your efforts with him over the years were simply to turn him into something so good that others stole him from you.

Perhaps it is good riddance? Perhaps if Terry has so little decent feeling that he can look back at six years of working together, six years of mutual trust and respect – yes, and even of affection – and turn his back on all that, then are you not better off without him?

You may be able to rationalise along those lines, but it still hurts, doesn't it? What happened to good old-fashioned loyalty? Is it dead?

Sooner or later in my Management Clinics when we are sitting around, perhaps during one of the breaks, chewing the fat and solving every management problem there ever was (and some that haven't been thought of yet), someone will bring up the topic of staff loyalty. He may say happily: 'We have a really strong sense of company loyalty in our team. Our staff turn-over is less than two per cent.' Or he may mutter angrily: 'There's damn little loyalty in employees these days. The first sign of trouble and they leave the company in droves.'

The group will generally come down on one side of this discussion or the other. Either they will say, yes, they too enjoy a good sense of loyalty in their staff or yes, they too find that the good old virute of loyalty seems to have been eroded by modern values. They may disagree with each other about whether staff loyalty is strong or weak, but not one of them ever seems to question the *existence* of such a quality as loyalty to the company by its employees.

I usually sit and listen to the discussion as long as

I can stand it, then I ask something like this: 'Will each of you think now of one member of your team who is really good at his/her job. He is good enough to be able to get a job with another company with no trouble at all. Has everyone got that person in his mind? Remember, he would have no difficulty in walking into another job tomorrow. Yet he stays with you.' Then I ask: 'Why? Why is he staying with you?'

After some hestiation, answers begin to come. I have done this exercise many times and the answers are always very much the same. I don't lead the group into certain answers by asking trick questions; I simply say: 'He could go, but he stays. Why?' Here are the sort of answers I get, every time:

1. His present salary is better than he will get elsewhere.

2. The future for him in this company is brighter – or he has reason to think do.

3. Fringe benefits (leave conditions, pension fund, company assistance in home buying and so forth) are better where he is.

4. The company has never missed a year-end bonus in twenty-four years.

5. He is used to the people he works with and is uncertain of what he would find if he moved.

6. The location of the company offices is conveniently near to his home, and clubs, schools, friends are all close by.

7. He fears to change – the feeling that the grass merely *looks* greener on the other side of the fence keeps him from moving.

That's how it always seems to end up, sometimes almost word for word. By now the more perceptive members of the group have shut up and are sitting listening to the others, who are still involved in finding answers. Those who have seen where the answers are heading catch my eye and grin. Then I say: 'Thank you. These are the reasons, the only reasons you can think of, that are keeping your employee with the company when he could easily go elsewhere. Tell me – just what has any of that to do with *loyalty*?'

Well, that little exercise does not make me very popular with some of the group, although I don't do it to score points over anyone. Nor do I do it so that they will henceforth look at all their employees with suspicious and jaundiced eyes, wondering who will be the next to leave as soon as the above considerations no longer apply.

The object of the exercise is simple. I am merely trying to stop a manager, when a member of his staff says that he has had another offer and is therefore leaving, from beating his breast and crying: 'Great balls of fire – is there no such thing as staff loyalty any more?' Or, even worse, from going into Gloom mode and agonising over his own deficiencies as a manager who can't even keep his staff.

The point is that we get good people and we lose good people. It is part of the flux of growth and move-ment in a business environment. People will stay while the seven points we have examined, or points similar to them, are working for us; they will leave when the points start working against us. When they do leave a company it does not mean that they are being 'disloyal'; it does not necessarily mean that their managers have failed them in some way: it does not necessarily mean that there is anything personal about it.

A valued staff member has told you that he is leaving? Very well, you do your best to find out if the decision has anything to do with a deficiency in the company policies or working conditions, or management philosophy or strategy. You make sure that he knows what he is leaving and what he is joining. Then you wish him luck.

If any manager falls into the simple error of crying out: 'Oh, Terry, isn't there such a thing as loyalty any more?' then Terry is likely to say: 'I'm sorry, Peter, but my first loyalty must be to myself and my family.'

And just what answer is there to that?

There are things which we can expect from a member of our work force. We can expect a fair day's work for a fair day's pay. We can expect him to be a good Public Relations Officer for the company, so that he projects a good company image at all times. We can expect him not to cause alarm and despondency among his fellow workers – not to be a troublemaker. Now if anyone would like to call these things indications of loyalty I won't argue, although they represent a very low grade of loyalty; to me they are simply aspects of the job we are paying him to do.

Here's a bone to throw to anyone who hates what he has just read, who believes that I have been talking through my hat. There *can* exist in a business organisation a very fine type of loyalty. It is a *personal* loyalty, and it exists between a manager and the members of his team. It can live only on a two-way basis and it is a priceless thing. It blossoms and is nourished by mutual trust, confidence, affection and esteem, and it creates a working relationship which money can't buy. It has however nothing whatever to do with the company.

If you still doubt me I don't blame you. It is not easy to let go of such a comforting myth as company loyalty. I have a client company, an insurance concern, with a very fine record of the way it treats its staff. I remember that after our Clinic we went on talking for two hours about this subject. Most of the managers attending found it too bitter a pill to swallow, and some of them have never forgiven me for the stand I take on this subject.

Two things to wind up this section, then. Loyalty to a company? But just what is a company? It is often said that 'A company is its people', but this is one of those time-worn clichés which is simply nonsense. The *strength* of a company may be its people, certainly, but a company is a bunch of shareholders who have bought a piece of the company for one reason and one only, and that is to make as much money as they can out of it. Now, how on earth can one think it necessary, desirable or even logical to have any loyalty to those people?

Lastly, remember the seven points we looked at earlier. Turn back to them and read them again. Ask yourself if they do not apply equally well to *you* as they do to your employee. Are they not the reasons, perhaps expressed in a more sophisticated, high-level way, that keep you in your present job? They don't have much to do with loyalty now, do they?

Loyalty to a company is a myth. Accept that as a fact. Every single person in any business entity is there because at this precise moment it suits him to be there, and if circumstances change sufficiently he will walk away without a backward glance. If in the future he ever has any warm feelings about the job he left it will be about the people he worked with, not the company.

'Is there no such thing as company loyalty any more?'

No, my masters – and there never was.

9

The old stager

Sam Oldguard is the Plant Manager of Alphabet
Motors. His job and his responsibilities are those of
workshop foreman, but in view of his long record of
good service the directors decided to give him the title
last year when they handed over his gold watch for
thirty years in the company. He is not qualified for the
job – he holds only a fitter's ticket – but so far his long
experience has made up for the lack of letters behind
his name.

Leslie Tring joined the company eighteen months
ago as Service Director. Highly qualified, he had three
years in another factory as assistant engineer before
joining Alphabet. He is twenty-eight years old; just
about half Sam Oldguard's age.

Sam was a tremendous help to Leslie when he
joined the company; he spent long hours in the
evenings and over weekends showing Leslie the ropes.
Even if he was a bit of a bore when he reminisced about
'the old days' when 'you knew what was what' he
was worth listening to when he talked about company

procedures and problems, customers and products. He adopted a fatherly attitude towards Leslie, until Leslie had to point out fairly firmly that he was the Service Director, and while he would permit 'Leslie', 'Young un' was not a suitable form of address.

Leslie has had the sort of problems to be expected when a younger person has to manage older people, but up until now he believes that he has handled these with the right mixture of tact and authority. Now he has a problem which threatens to nullify all the progress he has made so far with Sam Oldguard. The company has recently programmed its computer to include Work In Progress information. This entails the feeding in of all parts and accessories details and charges, as well as expected completion dates, deadlines, number of man-hours consumed, and all the minutiae which computer programmers love so much. A special form has been produced which has to be completed each day on each job, and it is this form which is the focus of trouble in the Alphabet Motors Service Division. Sam Oldguard took one look at it and flatly refused to have anything to do with it. 'Bloody silly waste of time. The old way was good enough for thirty years and it's still good enough. I'll have none of this new-fangled rubbish in my shop.'

Leslie Tring has had to be part diplomat, part dictator and part salesman to persuade Sam to accept the new form and the system that goes with it. For a time it seemed that he had been successful and apart from a few sarcastic remarks from Sam the system seemed to have been accepted by the department. Then the gremlins took over, and a combination of an improperly-trained programmer and some misfiled floppy discs created the sort of log-jam which systems analysts encounter in nightmares.

The problem has at last been sorted out but while it was still boiling away the workshop had to go back to the old way of recording jobs, using the old forms. When at last everything was working smoothly again one thing was still giving trouble – Sam Oldguard. He was now adamant that he was finished with the computer and everything and everyone connected with it. He had been heard to say in the canteen: 'Either that bloody pansied-up typewriter goes or I do.' Many of the artisans, especially the older ones, nodded their heads at this; they don't like the new forms and system either.

Leslie Tring has been told by the managing director to get his department back on the computer without delay. He is sitting in his office waiting for Sam Oldguard to come in for a talk which was set for three o'clock; it is now nearly three-fifteen. Leslie can see Sam through his glass partition; he is talking to two of the cleaning staff. He has glanced once or twice in Leslie's direction. Finally he laughs at something one of the cleaners has said and slowly makes his way to Leslie's office.

Sam: All right then, Leslie. What is it?

Leslie: Please close the door and sit down, Sam.

Sam: No need; I can't be staying long. I'm needed in the shop.

Leslie (Gets up and closes the door): Sit down, Sam.

Sam (With exaggerated patience): What is it, then.

Leslie: The computer is working again, all the problems have been sorted out, and we can now go back to using the new form. These forms (he taps a pile in front of him) are the old ones and the programmers can't use them to feed into the computer. Please take them away and transfer the information to the new forms.

Sam: You don't know what you are asking! It will take more than an hour to do that!

Leslie: Yes, I know it will, but you also knew four days ago that we were supposed to start using the new forms again and for four days now you have ignored that instruction. Here you are, and please have them back before you leave tonight.

Sam: Now, listen here–

Leslie: No, Sam, *you* listen. You ignored a clear instruction. That instruction doesn't come from me, it comes from the managing director himself. If you don't obey that instruction I will get it in the neck from the corner office, and I don't intend to take it. Here (he tosses the batch of cards across), have them back by five.

Sam: Look here, young un–

Leslie: My name is Mr Tring. You can call me Leslie.

Sam: Hoity toity! All right, Leslie; I'll tell you straight why I won't use the new forms. It's for the good of the company, and that's the truth.

Leslie: The good of the – what are you talking about?

Sam: The good of the company. Do you know how much overtime we had to pay for when that bloody computer thing broke down? And how many jobs were delayed? And how many customers were offended?

Leslie: I know all that, but–

Sam (Well into his stride now): Why, I had dozens of old customers phoning me at home, pleading with me to get their jobs through and damn the computer!

Leslie (Sceptically): Dozens of customers phoned you at home?

Sam: Yes!

Leslie: Such as who, for instance?

Sam (Brushing it aside): I didn't keep a list of them. Now, the company can't afford to have that sort of thing happening, can it now, young – Leslie?

Leslie: No, it can't and it won't happen again.

Sam: Ah, but who says it won't? They're always going wrong, those computers. Neighbour of mine, now, got a telephone bill for over five hundred quid, and he hadn't even been at home that month! He had the telephone people in to test–

Leslie (Raising his voice over the flow of words): Sam! I don't want to hear about it. The fact is that you will use the new forms from this moment on and I don't want any more from you about it.

Sam: And if I don't?

(There is a pause. The two men look at each other across the desk.)

HOW DOES IT LOOK SO FAR?

Well, Leslie has reached a crisis point. He can't duck the question Sam has asked (and he realises that it is less a question than a challenge) and how he answers it can affect the running of the Service division, the future of Sam Oldguard in the company and, to an extent, Leslie's future as well.

How does it seem to you? Has Leslie handled the interview efficiently so far? Efficiently, that is, not effectively, since he hasn't achieved anything worthwhile yet. Has he made his point clearly and firmly enough, while also taking into account Sam's good record, and his unstinting help when Leslie was still finding his feet?

You may feel that he has done reasonably well so far, considering what a (let's face it) pigheaded old warhorse Sam is. Or is he pigheaded, really? Why has he turned his face against the idea of the computer? Well, why have so many of the older generation all over the world done exactly the same thing? It needs no psychological expertise to know that the real reason is fear. This fear may stem from different roots; it may simply be the fear which comes from ignorance, and the feeling that they are the old dogs who are now incapable of learning new tricks. Younger people learn about bytes and interfacing and modems in school these days, and they come out into a world where the computer is a familiar and vital accessory to daily living. Older people look at the graphics magically taking shape on the screen and shrink from having anything to do with this monster.

Then of course there is the fear of dat ol' debbil de machine taking over someone's job. This is the fear which drove the Luddites to smash industrial machinery in the early part of the nineteenth century. Not that Sam believes that the computer will ever replace him, surely; but is it not possible that he sees it as making his job less important?

110

And then there is the simple but universal fear of change. Even when the change is probably for the better people often resist it; any officer in charge of a unit of soldiers knows that his men can be in the worst possible conditions, but when they have got used to those conditions and unless there is imminent danger they will resist moving to another position. In Sam's case he doesn't see any advantage for himself in the change and it interferes with the way he has been doing things for years and years. He was comfortable with the old way; he is uncomfortable with the new.

Finally the old, almost primitive fear that life has passed us by, that we have missed the boat, that it's too late. Sam Oldguard is fifty-six eyars old and he is not stupid; he knows that the title of Manager was handed over to him with his gold watch as a sign of affection and recognition of service, not as an indication that he is in any way an executive. He is a foreman, and when he retires he will still be a foreman. Here is this youngster Leslie Tring, about the same age as Sam's children, sitting in the swivel chair behind the desk and handing out orders, while he sits in the straight chair in front of the desk, taking the orders.

It is this last fear which often leads to apparently illogical behaviour on the part of the older person in business, and as I say, you don't need a degree in psychology to detect it, understand it and even sympathise with it.

All right, end of the amateur lecture on irrational behaviour. Did you detect any weaknesses in Leslie's management of the situation? There was one spot where he said completely the wrong thing – or said it in the wrong way. It was only one sentence but it was weak management. He said: 'This instruction doesn't come from me, it comes from the managing director himself. If you don't obey the instruction I will get it in the neck from the corner office.'

Bad. Very bad. This is hiding behind the skirts of the big boss, saying: 'Don't blame me, it's not my fault, I'm suffering here just as much as you are.' When a manager receives an order from the top brass to pass down the line it becomes *his* order with *his* authority behind it. To go back to a military analogy, no sergeant says to his platoon: 'The Captain has told me to tell you to take that hill. Now, this isn't my idea, so if you get killed don't come running to me.' No, he says: 'You will take that hill by 0715 hours. We move at 0700.' That's it; it is *his* order, whether he believes it or not. Apart from that one slip we might feel that Leslie hasn't done too badly, but now comes the crunch. Leslie has given Sam a direct order, and Sam has said: 'And if I don't?'

Leslie (Quietly): I don't think you mean that, Sam. I don't think that you and I want to fight each other over this. You have a record of solid service to this company which nobody can equal from the top to the bottom. Top management has more deep respect for you than you realise, and as for me, why, you were a valuable member of this company while I was in prep school! You know I look to you for the experience which I don't have. Now I can't believe that you want to throw all that away.

Sam: You are saying that if I don't knuckle under I'll be throwing all that away. Is that what you mean?

Leslie (Irritated): Damn it, Sam, there's no question of your 'knuckling under'. Please stop looking at this thing as though we were fighting a duel. (He takes a breath. Calmer) The computer is a fact of life. You don't like the way it seems to be intruding on your job. Well, I must tell you that the first time I heard that our records were going on computer my heart fell into my boots. Now that I know more about what it will do for us I realise that we can't do without it, and it is as simple as that.

Sam: We have done without it for–

Leslie (Firmly): Sam, don't start that again. We have been all over this before. We did without it – all right, *you* did without it when you had four journeymen, seven pieces of equipment and six hundred and forty different part numbers. You now have twenty-one workers, three shops full of equipment, and oh, Lord knows how many part numbers–

Sam: Four thousand, seven hundred and forty-one.

Leslie: You see? You see the sort of knowledge you carry around in your head? Sam, in your heart you are an Alphabet Motors man. I don't believe that you don't feel strongly enough about your life here not to go along with a direct policy decision, one which in the long run can only benefit you, me, and all those men of yours out there in the plant (Sam looks doubtful). Look, Sam – let's do these forms together right now. I'll enter the dope while you sing it out. It won't take a moment if we both do it. From tomorrow I'll get Helen Moffett to report to your office sharp at eight-thirty every morning and you can do them with her; that way it will take less than thirty minutes. What do you say?

Sam (Pinching his ear): –

Well, what would Sam have said? Let's leave that

cooking while we examine Leslie's progress so far. In this section we can, I think, congratulate him on defusing a potentially explosive situation. When Sam said: 'And if I don't?' He was throwing down the gage; unmistakably, he was daring Leslie to do his worst.

How easy it would have been for Leslie to hurl at Sam: 'If you don't then you are fired!' We could find it in our hearts to condone and even to applaud such a reaction. After all when you boil it all down, Sam has been more than a little bloody-minded about the whole affair. He has flouted the authority of his direct superior and even worse, perhaps, he has been inciting his subordinates to disobedience. This is not what we expect from a manager, and if Leslie had lost his temper and fired Sam then and there it would have been an action which could easily have been justified to senior management.

So, all praise to Leslie; he acted with a restraint and wisdom beyond his years and experience. He also did a very neat job of drawing teeth there, did you notice? He must have known that in Sam's mind was the thought that he was a part of Alphabet Motors when Leslie was still fighting his way through The Cat Sat on the Mat. Now, it only takes a confrontation such as this for the bile of jealousy and disappointment to burst out, and Sam could easily have said something which Leslie could simply not overlook, whereupon the situation could have been irretrievable. Some things said in anger can alter a relationship for ever – or end it. So Leslie said it first, and it was the best thing he did in the whole interview.

The last piece of good negotiation was Leslie's offer to Sam of a helper every day so that the routine of filling in the forms would be minimised. Much more important than the saving of a few minutes of Sam's time, though, was the fact that Sam was *getting* something from the exchange as well as giving something. It softened the order and made it more of a give-and-take thing – a salve to Sam's injured pride; a way to save face.

Can we now listen to Sam's answer?

Leslie: – From tomorrow I'll get Helen Moffett to report to your office sharp at eight-thirty every morning and you can do them with her; that way it will take less than thirty minutes. What do you say?

Sam (Pinching his ear): Oh, all right, then (Suddenly he grins and winks). All right, young un!

Leslie (Grins back): All right, old un!

10

'You are fired!'

An important section in my Management Clinics is Staff Selection, which is a look at the mysteries of hiring the right people. Because of my deep conviction that this could just be the most important of all management skills, we spend a lot of time on it. During one of these Clinics after we had handled the content of the subject, one of the delegates said: 'Yes, very interesting and of course, very important. Tell me, Michael, why do you have a section on Hiring yet no section on Firing?

And what a good question it is, too. If you have never had to dismiss anyone you may not realise what a disturbing and even traumatic thing it can be, and so often we walk away from the experience with the unhappy feeling that we blew the whole thing in one way or another.

Firing a member of our staff is one duty which we would dearly like to delegate to someone else. Indeed this is often done, with the manager chickening out and giving the job to an unfortunate subordinate, while the manager suddenly finds it necessary to visit an outpost of his empire that day.

Never do this. As managers we can delegate many aspects of our jobs, but not this one. A golden rule here (I've only just made it up and I don't know why I didn't think of it years ago) is: if you hired him, you fire him.

The reason that we are so reluctant to fire anyone (apart from a natural reluctance to dismiss someone with whom we have had a working relationship) is simple. When I have to get rid of a member of my staff I am saying loud and clear: 'I have failed with this person. My job was to manage him in such a way that he conformed to certain standards and attained certain levels of performance. He has not done this and I have therefore failed in the job I am expected to do.' The manager may not actually articulate this, but it is in his guts all the same, and it is an unpleasant meal to digest.

It isn't as bad as it sounds. The truth may be that no manager in the world could have done what was required with this person, so it is not necessary to assume any deficiency in the manager's managing of him; nevertheless there is failing there, and it is one of the reasons we flinch from getting rid of people.

Another reason, perhaps the most important, is the problem of confrontation. I talked to a young manager who seemed to be in a state of shock, and when I commented on his appearance he said that he had that morning gone through a horrifying experience. The day before, after much agonising and self-examination, he had dismissed one of his staff. He laid out the reasons behind his decision and action for me and they seemed to be good. In this case there was no alternative, the man had to go. That morning the man's wife had turned up at the company's premises and had burst into the manager's office, crying and wailing and pleading for her husband's reinstatement so that their two children could go on eating. What really turned this melodrama into a sort of ghastly burlesque was that she was dragging one child by the hand and had a screaming infant on her hip. The manager's face was grey as he recounted the scene. 'My God, I don't ever want to go through that again.'

If he remains a manager he may well have to, although perhaps not to that extent. We have all had tears on the other side of our desks, and not only from the strong sex – men cry too.

So. We all hate firing but it is part of the business of managing. Let us at least try to do it so that as little blood is shed as possible and so that we come out of the other end feeling that we have done an unpleasant job as well as may be.

WHY FIRE HIM?

How we conduct a dismissal interview depends almost entirely on the reason for the dismissal, so it makes sense to examine these reasons, together with some guidelines on what the tone of the interview should be.

1.   *Dishonesty*

Theft, embezzlement, fraud, whatever – he has been caught ripping the company off (or stealing from his workmates or colleagues) and you have decided not to give him another chance but to get rid of him.

In one way this case is the simplest of all. After all, he has been caught out in a crime, and unless there are mitigating factors such as hardship and dire need, there is no reason for compassion and you can simply go ahead. The other side of the picture is that you are accusing him of a crime and giving this as the reason for dismissal, and these days this could lead to more trouble than you have ever experienced as a manager. If you handle this one badly you may find that the employee who has been selling company tools and equipment or going through the lockers of his fellow workers has hauled you in front of a board, tribunal, committee or even court, and is about to collect enough from your company to retire on.

Two things; first, make sure, and I mean *sure*, of the facts before you accuse anyone of anything. If you don't have proof that will stand up in court then for heaven's sake (or more important, for your own job's sake) walk like Agag. Second, and it should have been first, if you have the slightest doubt about the circumstances then discuss it with the experts. Your company probably pays a fat retainer to a law firm so let them earn it. They don't handle the dismissal interview, mind; you still have to do that, but they can hear what you intend to say and scream with horror if you risk letting the company in for expensive litigation and, even worse (and this will give your PRO a nervous tic for weeks), give the company the image of a nasty, people-squashing machine in the eyes of the public.

The interview itself should not be difficult. Simply set out the facts and show him that the company doesn't employ people who act this way. You are probably as mad as hell with him (you hired him; and this is a betrayal of your trust, damn it!) so warn yourself that losing your temper will gain you nothing and may lose you much.

2. *Malice*

We throw on this garbage pile any course of action taken with evil intent. Some examples could be: putting the company in a bad light through some deliberate deed, stirring up unrest in the staff as an *agent provocateur*, sexual harassment (a very 'in' offence these days), actively eroding the authority of his superiors – all that sort of thing. Here again, the dismissal interview should present no great difficulty. We lay the facts before him dispassionately. We are perfectly willing to allow him to put his side of the case and listen carefully in case something should come to light which we have not been aware of and if nothing comes out of his part of the discussion, dismiss him.

Here's a point of contention: when you fire someone do you make him work out his time, or do you let him go immediately, paying him for the statutory period of his notice? Ask this question of a group of managers and you might as well bring out the boxing gloves. One school of thought says, hell, make him work out his time; why give him a paid holiday? The other school says, get him out of here before he infects the rest of the staff with his poison – and anyway if I see him just once more I'm going to kill him.

It depends why he is leaving, of course, but I usually go along with the second school of thought. Having someone around the place who already has one foot outside it is a little like living with a man who has been condemned to be hanged next Tuesday; it can get grim.

3. *Lack of ability*

Here the reason is that he simply can't do the job.

We can assume that he has been exposed to whatever training courses and programmes the company provides for that particular job, and that he has been properly supervised, counselled and appraised. All to no avail; he does not meet the standards required. He is not intelligent enough, strong enough, deft enough, articulate enough, quick enough, presentable enough – he is just not enough, and you have come, reluctantly, to realise that he won't ever be. He is willing; there is no indication of laziness, lack of interest or motivation here; he just can't cut it.

I know that it is an over-simplification, but I always feel that we should be firing two people in this case; after all, who hired this character? Who carefully, objectively, and using all the techniques, systems, tests and methods which modern technology provides, decided in his wisdom that our hero was the right person for the job? Why don't we fire him too? He really blew it on this one. Easy to write, but I don't really mean it because if I did I would have had to fire myself more than once. Nevertheless, having to sack a person because of lack of ability is almost always the result of hiring without sufficient attention to the basic requirements of the job, or because we have promoted someone to a job for the idiotic reason that 'Bobby has been here longer than anyone else, and how can we put someone over his head who has less than half of his time with us?'

Whatever the reason for it, having to dismiss anyone because of lack of ability is a sad affair. My main objective in these circumstances has always been to let him go with as much of his self-respect intact as is possible. After all, the fact that he can't do job A does not mean that he isn't perfectly capable of doing job B, and perhaps we can show him that if only we had a job B opening we would never have let him go. Also any company worth its salt would, without assuming any legal obligation or responsibility, try its best to help him find a job B somewhere.

Having said that, let us not let any guilt feeling extend to going overboard in a letter of reference for him. If as an act of expiation or penitence we get all gushy about Bobby's capabilities, talents, personality, experience and overall saintliness, not only will we look like idiots for letting him go but the hyperbolic testimonial may succeed in getting him another job where he can't do what is expected of him, and he will be worse off than before because there will be another failure on his record.

4. Retrenchment

There has been a merger and we suddenly have two corrosion engineers and one corrosion engineer's job. Or we have stopped building mattamores, and Clarence has been a mattamore man for thirty-four years and he has no experience of building gazebos and at his age it is unrealistic to expect him to change. Or profits have dropped by eighteen point seven per cent and a mathematical guru in Planning has decided that the way to deal with this is to reduce staff by three point nine per cent. Or and or and or.

Of all the reasons for dismissing people this is the one which managers hate most. It isn't his *fault*, blast it; he is doing a competent job. There has probably been no slightest warning, and we have the job of calling him in and dropping the sky on his head. Here as much as in any of the others we have a moral obligation to do our very best to place him somewhere else. The person has given a piece of his life to the company and it is the least that we can do.

If the ethics of the situation don't soften the stone you call your heart, Mr Attila, then consider the pragmatics; any example of a company treating its people unfairly gets around incredibly fast, and if you think that you live in a big city then get a reputation for ruthlessness in this regard and you will find just how small a village you do inhabit. I know of one hotshot sales director who decided that the average age of his sales force was much too high, so he went around with his litttle hatchet and chopped off the heads of all salesmen over fifty. One month's pay and leave your car keys at Reception. That was some years ago, and do you know that the company in question still has problems when trying to hire good people? The word gets around. On the other hand there was an oil company in my town which found that its middle management was top heavy. In one fell swoop it put nearly thirty people into early retirement. Each person had a private and confidential interview with the chief executive officer of the company, and every one came out of it with a smile from ear to ear. The going-away present was much more than generous. How do I know the story? I heard it from at least four sources, which shows that good news gets around as well as bad news.

In the case of retrenchment, even more is it necessary for the person to leave with his self-esteem still in one piece. To feel the trauma that can occur when someone is retrenched, lean back now and pretend that tomorrow morning you are asked into your manager's office, and after clearing his throat and tugging at his collar, your boss tells you that company policy has been changed and your job no longer exists so, very sorry, and this is no reflection on your work, but that is the way it is, and we are sure that with your undoubted ability you will have no difficulty, and if we can help in any way, and I personally feel very bad about it but the decision was taken only after much thought–

It slowly dawns on you that all that verbiage translates into: 'You are fired!'

How would you feel? And right at this minute you are saying: 'Well, I would feel awful, but thank heaven it isn't going to happen to me.' *That is what the man would have said whom you are now retrenching.*

So take it very easy on him; he is about to go through the darkness of self-doubt, shame, and guilt which can haunt the good man who suddenly finds himself without a job.

Those then are the main reasons for terminating employment and, as we have seen, the manager's constant efforts must be directed at, first, coming away from the interview with a whole skin and, second, leaving the unfortunate person who has been dismissed with as good a taste in the mouth as possible.

A final horror story for any manager who has ever thought: well, Jeffrey is not the right man for the job and he probably won't ever be. However, let's not be hasty about firing him. Who knows, he may improve or with any luck he may leave of his own accord and that will solve the problem nicely. In the meantime we'll just let things ride. If you have ever thought that then this story from a big industrial concern is for you:

A manager was transferred to another branch, which meant that instead of hiring his own people he inherited a group of people who had been hired by his predecessor, something which often happens. He carefully went thorugh the personal files of his new group and watched them at work over the next few months, evaluating each person's weaknesses and strengths. He was left after this exercise with the feeling that on the whole the team was a sound one with the right people in the right places. There was one exception; Oscar Hoople was a square peg in a round hole.

The manager investigated Oscar's case more deeply. He had, it seemed, been shifted from another department to his present job at the instigation of the previous manager; perhaps he had found something worthwhile in Oscar which no-one else had been able to discover. Oscar, he learnt, had an unhappy domestic situation in that his wife had run away with an office colleague and had left Oscar with two small children.

Oscar's lack of ability made a good case for firing him, but the manager called on his reserves of humanitarian feeling and compassion and kept him on; how could you rub salt in the wounds of a man in his unfortunate position by throwing him out? He kept Oscar on for over four more years, with Oscar's work remaining at its less-than-satisfactory level. Finally the manager threw in the towel and called Oscar in to his office. he said: 'Oscar, I'm sorry; I would like to break this to you gently but there isn't any way to do it. I am going to have to let you go.'

Oscar was thunderstruck. 'Let me go? You are sacking me? Why?'

'Because you simply are not the right man for the job you do. You are basically a good rough worker, but your job calls for attention to detail, and on that side you just don't make it. I'm sorry, Oscar. When I came here four years ago I saw that you had this problem but I thought that if we persevered you would show an improvement. I have tried for four years and that is as far as I can go. You are going to have to leave. I'm truly sorry.'

Oscar Hoople stared at his manager in disbelief. 'You felt four years ago that I wasn't right for the job?'

'Yes, Oscar. I've been patient for all that time, but now–'

'You bastard!' Oscar's face was a mask of fury. 'You bastard! You have wasted four years of my life!'

Oscar Hoople was twenty-nine years old when his manager first thought of firing him because he was the wrong man for the job. Out of the kindness of his heart he kept him on. Oscar is now thirty-three years old. He now has to compete for a job with people still in their twenties. Now he is four years older, but no better, no bigger, no higher, than he was four years ago.

How kind can a manager be?

11

The perfect gentleman

Artie Manners has been on Dick Henty's sales force for nine months now. His sales figures have never been particularly high but now there is a definite downward trend, especially in new business volume.

Artie gets on well with people, both in the company and out in the field. His customers like him and in fact one customer telephoned Dick and complimented him on having a 'perfect gentleman' on his team.

Artie's reports are neat and comprehensive; perhaps a shade *too* comprehensive. He never gives any trouble, he is punctual, responsive to instructions, and a hard worker. If it wasn't for his sales figures he would be no worry at all, but now he seems to be reluctant even to make calls on prospective customers. He attends all sales meetings but does not participate unless asked a direct question, whereupon he stammers, blushes, and dries up after three words.

Although nobody knows where he got the courage to do so, he has asked a girl to marry him. The wedding takes place next month and Dick Henty has agreed to be best man.

Artie says he likes selling. 'I like the challenge and I like meeting people.' In a burst of confidence he once told Dick that he hoped one day to be worthy of the job of manager.

Dick Henty and Artie Manners are bent over forms at Dick's desk. The occasion is the half-yearly appraisal interview. In this company the employee is given a blank appraisal form and he has to appraise himself on a one to ten basis under various headings. He is given two days to do this – he is expected to do it in the evenings – and at the same time his manager is filling in an identical form. During the appraisal interview the manager and his subordinate discuss each heading and compare the gradings which each of them has put down. The interview between Dick Henty and Artie Manners has been in progress for twenty minutes.

Dick: What have you given yourself for Paperwork (Punctuality) and Paperwork (Content)?
Artie: Er – nine and eight, Dick.

Dick: No. Ten and ten. Your paperwork is *always* on time and *always* properly filled in.

Artie (Blushes): Well – thank you.

Dick: Don't thank me, and you are not supposed to be modest with your gradings. You are evaluating yourself as objectively as possible. Your mark for Product Knowledge?

Artie: Seven.

Dick: I have six, and even that's a bit high. We are

going to have to concentrate on some aspects of your P. K. What about Customer Knowledge?

Artie: Eight.

Dick: No, Artie; nowhere near eight. I have five.

Artie (Dismayed): Only five?

Dick: Artie, you do not know your customers. Your customer cards are always neat and they are always on time but they are not accurate because you don't have enough information to make them accurate (He flips a record card at Artie). Look at that one – Modern Fixtures PLC. You have your contact there as N. K. Hurst, right?

Artie: Well, yes, of course. I see him every time I call on Modern Fixtures.

Dick: Why?

Artie: Why do I call on him, Dick? Well, because he's the buyer, of course!

Dick: He is not the buyer. In the first place his name is not spelt Hurst, it's H-e-a-r-s-t. Artie, he is not the buyer.

Artie: But surely-

Dick: Norman Hearst is the chief storeman for Modern Fixtures. Why do you think that on the few occasions you have managed to get an order from Modern, the order is always less than £50 in value?

Artie: I know that they are small buyers, but the orders could get bigger, and I am working on Hearst.

Dick: The orders will *never* get bigger, for the simple reason that Norm Hearst has a buying limit of £50.

He is not *allowed* to spend more than that. You say that Modern are small buyers; do you realise that Brownings & Co. sells them more than £8000 every year? And do you know why that is? It is because the Brownings salesman calls on the *buyer* of Modern – and he is someone whose suite of offices is in the main building, not like Norman Hearst who sits in his cubicle in the factory drinking tea and chatting to you.

(Artie hasn't a word to say.)

HOW'S IT GOING SO FAR?

What do you think; is Dick Henty being a little hard on Artie Manners? He certainly didn't mince his words when showing Artie how little he knew about his customers. Couldn't he have done it a little less brutally though? Artie is obviously not a very strong personality, and isn't this sort of treatment just the way to make him crawl into his shell and never come out again?

Perhaps, but remember that this is a formal appraisal interview. Here a manager has the job of identifying and correcting weaknesses, recognising strengths, and setting goals and standards for the next six months. This is no cosy chat he is having with his man over a couple of jars on a Friday night. He is also, and this is important, reaffirming the relationship between himself and his subordinate; that is, he is setting the tone or attitude which will prevail between them from now on.

Dick as we can see has a middle-of-the-road

management pattern with his people. On the one hand he is on first-name terms with them and we feel that he encourages two-way communication in their meetings with him. On the other hand he has no hesitation about pointing out deficiencies in such a way that there can be no doubt in the salesman's mind as to how Dick feels about his performance. The interview continues:

Dick: Artie, that is what I mean by poor customer knowledge; you don't even know the name of the buyer of a potentially valuable customer.

Artie: I'm sorry, Dick. What is his name? I'll call on him tomorrow.

Dick: I'm not telling you his name. I want from you a complete and accurate list of all the purchasing officers of all the customers and prospects in your territory. I want it on this desk four weeks from today (He turns a page of the appraisal form). Staff Relations: I have marked you nine. You always get on well with the internal staff, you respect their problems and you don't waste their time.

Artie (Relieved that he seems to be doing something right): Thank you.

Dick: Stop thanking me. These marks are not a present from me to you, Artie. They are an estimate of your performance. Sales Volume. Artie, I don't know what you have marked for this section but if it is more than three, forget it (Artie looks unhappy; his marking must be more than three). Your sales curve over the last two months looks sick. What has happened?

Artie: Well, Dick, you know, the whole team has been having trouble with sales recently–

Dick: I'm not talking about the whole team, I'm

talking about you: however, if you have any thoughts about hiding behind the sales figures of the rest of the boys, have a look at these print-outs. Of the seven other men, three are holding their own, two are very slightly down and two are actually up. You are the exception. Your graph is dropping steadily. Why?

Artie (Really unhappy now): I don't know, Dick. I've thought and thought.

Dick: Have your thoughts led you to any conclusions?

Artie: Er – no.

Dick: All right, let's do some thinking together (he pulls a scratch pad towards himself). A salesman gets higher sales figures through several ways. First, he increases his 'Number of Sales' (writes it down) which is of course simply the number of people he has persuaded to buy in a given month (Artie nods, grateful that for the moment anyway he is not being sat on). Next he can raise his figures by bettering his 'Calls to Sales Ratio' (writes it down) which is his batting average, as it were, right?

Artie: Right!

Dick: Lastly, his figures go up when he increases his 'Average Order Value' (writes it down) which means that instead of getting a £250 order from a particular customer he increases it to £500. All clear?

Artie: Oh, yes.

Dick (Flips through the computer print-out sheets and pulls one out): Artie, here are your records for the last quarter. On each line the seventh figure is yours and the eighth is the company average. Run your finger along 'Number of Sales'. You are thirty-one per cent lower than the company average.

Artie: Oh.

Dick: The next line is 'Calls to Sales Ratio'. Company average is two point seven six to one. Yours is four point three five to one.

Artie (Stricken): Oh!

Dick: Next line, 'Average Order Value'. Company, which means all your team mates, £378. You, £231 (Artie has lost most of the colour in his face). There is one more way for a salesman to increase his sales volume, Artie. Do you have any idea what it could be?

Artie (Deep in despair): No, Dick.

Dick (Tapping the print-out): Here we are talking about *present* customers. That's all very well, and we have to stay close to them and call on them and give them good service; but what about *new* business? One of the best ways to make a sales graph go up instead of down is by prospecting, Artie! Now, the two top men in the team – you know who they are–

Artie: Ferdie and Martin?

Dick: Ferdie and Martin. Always at the top of the list, always win the awards. Why?

Artie: Well, they are just hotshots at selling.

Dick: I'll tell you what they are hotshot at. They are always looking for new business; they are great prospectors, Artie!

Artie (His worst fears are being realised. This is an

area he desperately hoped would not be brought up):
I – I suppose so.

Dick: *Believe* so. The consistently good salesman is the one who consistently looks for new business. Let's see your prospect list.

Artie (The axe is about to fall): I'm not sure that I–

Dick (patiently): Artie, if you don't have it with you then you are in deep trouble. Standing rules are that your prospect list stays closer to you than your Y-fronts. Hand it over (Artie fishes around in his briefcase and hesitantly hands over a single sheet of paper). *This* is your prospect list? (He gives it the briefest of glances, drops it on the desk and closes his eyes.)

Artie: I know it isn't quite up to date. There are a couple of names that I haven't yet– (He dries up).

Dick (Quietly): What am I going to do with you, Artie? If I had asked for your prospect list at the start of this interview I could have saved myself a lot of time and energy. This (he taps the offending sheet without looking at it) is the most damning indictment of a salesman that I have ever seen. Look at it. Eleven names – *eleven*! Not one of the rest of the team has fewer than fifty names. Ferdie has one hundred and twenty-five. The last name here was entered nearly a month ago. You have called on precisely three of these people in the past fortnight. What is it, Artie? What's the matter?

Artie (Shakes his head): I– (Nothing).

Dick: You grow prize geraniums, don't you?

Artie (Astonished): F – fuchsias.

134

Dick: Well, I don't know anything about gardening, but I suppose that if your fuchsias start acting up, losing their leaves or getting big black blotches all over them, you have a standard set of basics to check, like – hell, I don't know – are they getting too much water or not enough, are you using the right fertiliser, what about caterpillars or aphis – that sort of thing, right?

Artie (Mystified): Oh, yes.

Dick: Well, when one of my salesmen stops performing properly I do a similar check. My check goes something like this: One, Product Knowledge. If he doesn't know what he is selling he isn't going to sell. Now your product knowledge is not marvellous but that is not the problem. Next, Domestic Situation. Now, I don't like getting involved with the private lives of my people but sometimes it's inevitable. However, I saw Milly waiting in the car-park for you yesterday and from the big kiss you got I take it that everything is okay in that department.

Artie (Blushing): Oh, yes.

Dick: All right. Then, such items as Product Confidence, Staff Relations, your own health, which seems to be fine at the moment–

Artie: Yes, thank you.

Dick: Don't thank me, Artie, this is not a social occasion. Well, I go down the list with you in mind and I find nothing – nothing to show why your sales record is so bloody awful (Artie shakes his head to show that he, too, is baffled). The last item on my list is Bone Idleness (Artie looks shocked), but you don't qualify for that either. When you spent two weeks in the Order Department before you went on the road

Jock Norton told me that you were the most hard-working man he had ever had in Orders (Artie is about to thank Dick again, but the look on Dick's face stops him). So, Artie, I have come to the one conclusion that I didn't want to come to. I have walked round and round this, looking for an alternative and there is no alternative (He takes a deep breath). Artie, you are not a salesman.

Artie: Oh, Dick! I know I'm not very good at the moment, but I will improve, I promise you!

Dick (Holding up his hands): Artie, don't misunderstand me. I am not merely saying that you are not good enough right now; I'm telling you that selling is not for you (Artie goggles at him). One example only; do you remember that lead I gave you last month, the RFD Clothing Company? Do you remember I told you that I had met Ronald Burns at a Rotary meeting and that he had said that he would be pleased to see a salesman of mine and to hear the story on our product range?

Artie (Quietly): I remember.

Dick (Equally quietly): I reminded you three times to call on him, Artie. There was always some reason that you couldn't go. Eventually I had to send Mac. Now, that was the sort of lead that every salesman dreams of – an open door with someone expecting him and prepared to listen. You didn't make the call. You don't like calling on people, especially new people. You spend your working day calling on the few customers who have become your friends. You are always welcome there, because you don't bother them by trying to sell them anything; they consider you a perfect gentleman (Hits the desk). Artie,

Winston the lift man is a perfect gentleman – but he isn't on my sales team. I can't afford gentlemen; I need salesmen. I'm not talking about high-pressure people, I'm talking about assertive salesmen, and the word is assertive. You have some good things going for you, Artie, but you will not assert yourself. You are actually *afraid* to make calls – and a salesman who is afraid to make calls is not a salesman. You are not a salesman.

WHAT DO YOU THINK?

Well, it seems that Artie is on the point of being fired, and we needn't stay to watch the *coup de grace*.

What about it? Is Dick Henty giving up too easily? Is there not something he could do to save Artie? Remember our very first axiom: we don't have problems with bad people; we have problems with good people who have problems. Artie Manners is not *bad* in the sense of deliberate dereliction of duty, malice or idleness; he is a person in the grip of a fear which is keeping him from doing an adequate job. Well, that's not his fault. Can we point a finger at his manager and accuse him of neglecting Artie's development in any way? We can of course go back to the beginning of Artie's career with the company and ask why he was hired, but we are past that. Now we have to ask: can anything be done to save him?

What about training? Why not put him on an intensive training programme? Well, I am a trainer, so may I have a voice in this? My advice is, don't waste your money. Training won't help. You can't change a *personality* by training. Training does not change a person, it only develops what that person already has, and there is nothing in Artie that we can detect that can be developed. A shocking amount of time, money and effort is consumed in trying to turn people into something they are not.

When I was the training manager for a conglomerate I had one man in basic sales training who had only recently joined the company and was about to be assigned to a field job. My reports on him included the comment 'I do not believe that this man is tough enough for the battlefield of fast-moving consumables.' The report was read by one of our branch sales managers who had come up to head office for the purpose of selecting two new salesmen for his branch. Having interviewed our hero he came to my office.

'I think you are wrong about Fred Taylor,' he said. 'I think he can make it.'

I said: 'I'm often wrong about people, but I am on solid ground when I say that Taylor is not tough enough for fast-movings.' The manager asked me how, on the basis of a few days in a conference room, I could be so sure. I said: 'In discussion he would begin to make a point quite confidently, but as soon as he was challenged by one of the other delegates he would back down. Now, you know the sort of buyer he would have to face in the field in your area; they would argue with you about the Ten Commandments. How do you expect Taylor to hold his end up with that bunch of ruffians?'

We discussed Taylor further and I was as positive as I knew how that he would never make it, but the manager was adamant that I was wrong. 'I'll *make* him a good salesman,' he said.

Some eight months later I visited his branch on another matter, and he couldn't wait to wave Fred

Taylor's record under my nose. 'See? I was right!' he crowed. I had to admit that the sales figures were reasonably good; not wonderful, but adequate. I was still not convinced, however, and I did a little spying around the branch, more to see if I could find anything which would soothe my scratched ego than with any idea of changing anything. As I had half suspected, Fred Taylor's sales figures were correct, but most of the sales had been made with the manager going out with Fred Taylor and making the call with him. One of the other salesmen remarked: 'The boss spends more time with Fred than with any three of the rest of us.'

That was it. Determined to justify his choice of Fred or, more charitably, convinced that he could actually change him from a shy violet into a gladiator, the manager had been working with him far more than he should have with any one salesman. In the process, of course, you could say that he had been cheating the company, since it meant that he had been neglecting the other salesmen. Raise your eyebrows at that accusation if you like, but it is literally true.

WINDING IT UP

There comes a time when we have to stop fooling ourselves about whether or not we can make a person fit a job. In many cases we can trim off some sharp edges, rub down there, polish all over and generally mould a person so that he is more suitable for the specific requirements of the job. I say, in many cases we can, but he has to have the attitude and the capability first. If he has these then we can indeed develop them, and this is what a manager's job is all about.

Give a good manager someone with the 'Want to' and the 'Able to' and he will manage that someone so that he fits. Leave out one of those and the best manager in the world is helpless.

On the information we have in the case of The Perfect Gentleman it seems that Dick Henty did everything in his power to make Artie Manners a salesman. That he failed is not his fault; what is important to us is the fact that when the time came that he realised that he *had* failed, he did not stall or hesitate; he took immediate action.

If his tone in the interview seems to us rather cold and dictatorial perhaps we should take into account the natural disappointment of a manager who sees that he has used up a lot of time and effort on something which he is now compelled to write off. Also there was little point in sugar-coating the pill he was forced to administer to Artie. He was firing him for totally failing the job he was hired to do. Irrespective of any excuses, setting aside any blame or guilt, he had failed.

One good point for Dick Henty? Before he even began the interview he had every available fact at his fingertips, and oh, what a command of the situation this places in a manager's hands! One thing only was he short of and that was Artie's prospect list, and he couldn't get this without seeing Artie in person. Once he had this in his hands the case was complete and he could pronounce his verdict – and Artie's sentence.

To end on a happy note; in this actual case the company at Dick's suggestion decided to make use of Artie's strong points such as his capacity for hard work and his excellent paperwork. He was offered and gladly accepted the job of Sales Correspondent. Dick Henty's speech as best man at the wedding of Artie and Milly

Manners was a much more pleasant affair than the interview we have just examined.

12

From buddy to boss in one uneasy step

Until five weeks ago Terry Sanford was a salesman in the Durable Consumer Division of Pinnacle Electrics Company. He was part of a happy team which worked more or less effectively under Clarence Trotter, the long-time Division sales manager. The team had no inspired crackerjack salesmen in its ranks but neither were there any misfits, and the sales volume was generally satisfactory if not very exciting.

Then Clarence Trotter had a mild heart attack in the office during a sales meeting. Although he recovered well the experience was enough to make him realise that man is mortal, and the urging of his wife and the recommendation of his doctor were enough to make him go to the Board and seek early retirement.

This caught senior management quite unprepared. They had thought that they had at least five years to go before having to make any decision about a successor for Clarence; now they had to find one in a month. They cast around in a panic and decided that the best qualified man in the team was Terry Sanford.

At the management meeting during which this decision was made the Sales Director took the floor to make a statement.

'Trotter's retirement could be the best thing that happened to the Durable Division,' he said. 'Old Clarence was all right and he has given Pinnacle many years of faithful service, but I have been feeling for some time that he was over the hill.'

'You never said so,' said the managing director.

'No, because there wasn't very much we could do about it. We couldn't fire Trotter but at the same time we couldn't motivate him to get off his bum and put some fire into his team. I have been watching Durables for some time and while I know that the sales figures have been on quota I believe that we have been letting Clarence Trotter get away with a quota which was far too low.'

'He was always able to justify it at the annual sales conference,' said the chief accountant.

'Yes, I know he was, but when you think about it you realise that Clarence was a smooth-tongued character, and I think that if he put his mind to it he would have been able to justify putting Mrs Tiggy-winkle on the sales force. What I think we have in Durables now,' said the sales director, 'is Sheltered Employment. I don't think that those men are working hard enough, for the simple reason that they don't *have* to work very hard in order to make quota.'

'What do you propose to do about it?' asked the M. D.

'We have decided that Sanford gets the job,' said the sales director. 'Very well, then he has good news and bad news. The good news is the office, the secretary, the classy car, the title and the bumped-up salary. The bad news is that the easy times are over for the durable Consumer Division of Pinnacle Electrics. From the next fiscal year, which as you know starts in seven weeks, Durables' overall quota goes up one-third.'

'Are you going to let him hire more salesmen?' This from the personnel manager, who saw more work for her department.

The sales director shook his head. 'He can hire one more man to replace himself in the field and that is it. Durables is going to get out of neutral and into overdrive.'

Five weeks later then, that is the situation which faces Terry Sanford. After chewing over the position at some length but to little avail, he has decided to hold a sales meeting. This will be the second meeting he has held with his new team, although the first could hardly be dignified by the title 'meeting', since it consisted mostly of his team congratulating him on his new job and it ended with him buying several rounds of drinks at the pub around the corner.

Terry Sanford realises that this meeting will be a very different affair from the first happy bunfight. The days of wine and roses are over, and he is faced with a difficult task. How is he to get across to his old buddies that the company has suddenly started demanding more from the Division? Can he exert authority on and expect obedience from the happy band of drummers who were once his mates? For the first time Terry realises the truth of the saying, 'Promotion is like a corkscrew; to go up it is best to go around'. How much easier it would have been if, instead of promoting him directly upwards over his own team, the company

144

had moved him to another area, or even another division!

However, those are daydreams; today is harsh reality. Terry has called his meeting and is waiting for his team to turn up. He hopes that everyone will be on time, so that he won't have to tramp on someone right at the start of the meeting or, perhaps even worse, have to ignore a direct breach of discipline.

The whole team of six men turns up exactly on time. This is a relief to Terry until he realises that for all of them to arrive at the same moment means that they have probably come from somewhere together, and he wonders which coffee-house they have come from and what they have been discussing there. He feels that the subject was probably Terry Sanford, new Division sales manager. They take their seats and Terry stands up at the head of the conference table. He has a set of pre-drawn transparencies for the overhead projector.

Terry: Well, good afternoon and thanks for coming.

Dan (Falsetto): Thanks ever so much for inviting us! (It gets a titter from the group.)

Terry: I have just had the sales quotas from Mr Henderson and I thought you should see them as soon as possible.

Dan: Oh-oh. Just a minute while I get my heart pills out. My doctor says I shouldn't be exposed to shocks.

Terry (Mildly): Shut up, Dan. Now here (He switches on the OHP) is the overall figure for all products for the coming year, compared with the figure for this year (All six men are staring at the screen; they seem to have gone into shock). Now here is the total figure

145

broken down into products (He switches on and shows a new transparency, and now the team has found its collective voice:

From the floor: Wha-a-a-at?
Has management gone out of its mind?
You can't be serious!
That is a *one-third* increase!
Switch it off; I can't stand to look at it!
- And so on. Terry waits until the tumult and the shouting has died).

Terry: Those are the figures and it's no good crying about them. Management has decided that this Division is going to get those figures in the next twelve months or else.

Johnny: Or else what?

Terry (Hesitates): Well, or else there will be some unhappy faces around the boardroom table.

Johnny: Which means that there will be an unhappy face in the office next door to this one (The office next door is Terry's new abode).

Terry (Quietly): Yes, Johnny, that's right (Terry recalls that Johnny was the one man who did not clap him on the back and pump his hand when news of his promotion became known; also he made an excuse and did not come to the pub for drinks).

Johnny: Wouldn't look very good, would it – Clarence Trotter has an unbroken record of meeting quota, and the new boy screws it up in his first year.

WHAT IS HAPPENING HERE?

What is happening here is a potential showdown, and the team is not slow in realising that there could be a shoot-out between Johnny Farlow and Terry Sanford. Johnny, as it happens, was the other man on the Board's short list for the job, and only his acerbic manner blocked his choice – management felt that he would antagonise his subordinates with his biting tongue.

It seems that he understands that he was passed over for Terry – he would have to be very insensitive not to guess this – and it also seems that he is now preparing to sabotage Terry's first efforts at managing. This situation is understood by everyone in the room, and since everyone likes a good Western, they are settling down for a re-enactment of the Gunfight at the O. K. Corral. A lot depends on how Terry handles this situation right now.

Terry (Sits on the edge of the conference table): Let's talk about Clarence, since Johnny has brought up the subject. I think we all know how the company felt about him. He was a good company man and everyone respected him. He was a good manager to everyone in this room, and to many of us he was a good friend. He–

Rex: You sound as though he was dead. Why the obituary?

Terry: No, he isn't dead, but I am going to make a point about the last few years of his running this outfit. I believe that management didn't push Clarence too hard for those last few years; I think that they more or less let him run on a long leash. Now that

147

meant that we, his sales team, also had it pretty easy. Come on now, fellows; can anyone honestly say that he has had a tough time making quota this year, for instance?

Linford: We were not exactly loafing, Terry.

Terry: No, Lin, nobody is accusing us of loafing, but we were not what you could call flat out, either.

Johnny: You can speak for yourself; I worked hard this year. If you dragged your feet then that's your concern, not ours. Perhaps taking it easy is the formula for success around here, anyway, since it got you Clarence's job.

The dusty street is deserted. The two figures face each other, hands hanging close to their Colt Peacemakers. Faces appear at windows. The theme tune from 'High Noon' fades down and out.

Terry: Johnny, you asked for this: that bull about how hard you worked this year. Everyone knows how you go to the races every Wednesday and play squash every Tuesday and Thursday. Just because you – (he stops at the very edge of the abyss. Another half-dozen words and the hands would have leapt for the six-shooters and blood would have stained the dust. Had Terry finished the sentence – 'Just because you expected to get the job instead of me' – one of two things would have had to happen. Either Johnny would have had to resign or Terry would have had to apologise immediately in the presence of the whole sales team, and would thereby have put himself in a position from which he may never have recovered).

Johnny (Calmly): Yes? Just because?

148

Terry: Just because you made quota doesn't mean you were doing a full day's work (Very quick, that. Everyone in the room breathes again). Now, as I was saying, the top brass took it easy on Clarence. He has gone, and with him have gone the easy days for this division. You don't have to believe me, just believe the figures. I have only shown you the breakdown for products. Here (he switches on another transparency) are the breakdowns by territory. Any comments or questions?

Terry came so close to blowing it. There may be good reasons and justifications for losing your cool with a subordinate in private, but it is a very seldom thing (if ever) that we can start a shouting match with him in public. I said that everyone likes a good Western, but the fact is that if Terry and Johnny had really reached for their guns it would have had a bad effect on the group. A good working group is like a family, in that it realises that in-fighting can only weaken the whole fabric of its existence, and it tends to avoid open breaks whenever it can. You may have experienced this in a group of your own, that the group itself will reject the troublemaker just as an animal group will expel the rogue male, because he jeopardises the security of the group. It is as true in the human as in the animal kingdom.

Terry may have expected cries of horror and grief when he showed the transparency giving the territory quotas – which are, of course, also the individual sales-man's quotas. However, the screen was watched for the most part in silence, with one or two of the team making a few notes. After the big shock of the one-third increase the breakdown figures were expected. Also, and this is the real reason for the subdued tone in the room, Terry's remarks about having had it easy for the past few years have hit home. Salesmen know perfectly well when too much is being asked of them, but they also know when they are not working at full capacity, and each one in the group knows that this is indeed what has been happening. It must have occurred to the more intelligent of them that the situation could not last for ever, and perhaps now that the blow has fallen it has come as something of a relief. After all, it could have been worse; instead of getting everyone to work harder, management could have done some drastic chopping off of heads and gone out and hired a new team of *hardworking* salesmen. The group continues to study the figures.

Rex: My figure for Small Appliances seems high, Terry; these days that sort of thing – hair-dryers, grillers, kettles – sells more through the big chain stores than through the small electrical shops, and I don't have any big stores in my territory.

Terry: You don't now, Rex, but that shopping complex is opening in Sevenoaks in a few months and it will have two big stores in it; Williams and Tritex. You should do well with your sell-ins in both of them (Rex nods in acceptance). Anything else? (The group is beginning to make getting-up movements.) Wait a minute, fellows. We haven't finished yet, by a long chalk (Johnny, having risen, remains standing with an exaggerated look of patience on his face). Johnny, sit down (Johnny sighs loudly and sits).

The next ten minutes could be the most important of Terry Sanford's career in Pinnacle Electrics. He has had the title of Divisional Sales Manager for five weeks but until this moment he has not really done any *managing*.

Now he has the job of nailing his set of standards up on the wall and of getting them recognised, accepted and acted upon by his new team. *What* he has to do is obvious; *how* he goes about doing it is of the utmost importance in his future dealings with the group. Hamlet's mother, the Queen, pleaded for 'More matter, with less art.' Not so here. Here the art is vital, for without it the matter won't get across at all; not now, not ever.

Terry (Smiles at Johnny): Chum, you and I locked horns for a moment back there. Let's forget it. What we have got to do now is more important than a passing irritation. Now, fellows. This big bump up in quota may look like bad news but in fact it is good news (The group doesn't look as though this fact has got through to them). The thing is that Consumer Durables has been the poor relation in Pinnacle for a long time now. We don't add anything worthwhile to the profits of the company, and I have the feeling that the only reason we haven't been shut down or sold off is that when old man Sunderland started up the business seventy years ago he was making electric irons in the back room of his cottage. I don't know if any of you realise that the reason that our top steam iron is called the 'Maggie' instead of a model number is because Arnold Sunderland's wife was called Margaret.

So, perhaps we belong to a Division which has survived only through sentimental reasons. Now, that is not good enough, so we are going to show management that we can be a worthwhile and profitable part of this organisation (He takes a deep breath). We won't do it if we go on as we have been. That is not anybody's fault; there's no blame being fastened on anyone here.

We are going to have to change. The first thing to

change is the Call planning/Call reporting system (He passes out some forms). This is the revised system. As you can see I have incorporated the Planning and the Reporting forms into one. Every month you will fill in the Planner for the month to come and hand it in to me. It is printed on carbonless paper and the second sheet automatically becomes the Report sheet. At the end of the period you give me the second sheet, which by then you have filled in, and the third sheet you keep as your own record of both Planned Calls and Actual Calls made. What do you think?

Dan: Hell, Terry, it's much too complicated.

Ronnie: No, it isn't. As a matter of fact it's a lot less trouble than the old system. Nice work, Terry.

Terry: Thanks, Ron. Believe me, fellows, the last thing I want to do is load you with a lot of paperwork, mainly because the more you have to do, the more I have to do.

Morris (Who has not said a word up till now): Okay, if we have to do all this extra work let's get the hell out of here (The group begins stirring again).

Terry: Wait a minute; we haven't finished yet (The group is still getting papers together and talking amongst themselves). Wait! (He slaps the table loudly). This meeting is not over. You will stay here until I say you can go! (This outburst immediately shuts everyone up; they have not ever heard Terry talk like that.)

Terry (Quietly): That new form is merely one of the physical things which we are changing in this Division; there are others. First, the lunch-time snooker matches at Solly's are finished. No more. Understood?

Johnny: Now, just a minute there. When you were one of the peasants like the rest of us you played as much lunch-time snooker as anyone else. Now that you have been elevated to the bloody peerage, suddenly snooker is verboten. What kind of justice do you call that?

Terry: You are one hundred per cent right. I did play with the rest of you. I'm not proud of it or ashamed of it, it was just something which in the old days we used to do. *Used* to do. Not any more.

Dan: But that's lunch-time! That's on our own time. What's wrong with taking a break and getting together with your mates?

Terry: Dan, you know damned well what's wrong with it. Taking a break at lunch-time is fine, but getting together is not. How long does it take you to get from your territory to Solly's?

Dan: Oh, not more than ten minutes.

Terry: That's from the nearest part of your territory; I'm talking about the middle, the average, and it's nearer to half an hour. That means over an hour a day wasted, because you get to Solly's at one o'clock and you never leave until after two, as well as all that mileage in company transport. No, make no mistake, if I find that you people have been getting together at lunch-time from all over your territories there will be trouble (He looks around; there is no comment). Now, still on the subject of time, let's all of us get to the first call at eight-thirty in the morning. I know that most salesmen feel that because working hours are from eight-thirty to five they can leave their homes at eight-thirty and get back at five; they can't. Cyril, the chief order clerk, doesn't leave home at eight-thirty, he leaves home so that he arrives at work at that time, and he keeps on working until five. A good salesman does the same.

Last thing is these sales meetings. I know that Clarence used to hold them at this time – three o'clock every Friday – and at four we all used to go home. Now, that is a clear waste of a full afternoon every week and it is just not on. This is therefore the last meeting we have on a Friday. From now on, instead of a meeting every week which isn't necessary anyway, I am halving the number and we shall be having one every fortnight.

Dan: Damned good idea! (The others nod and murmur their approval. Terry smiles grimly to himself; the next piece of news will not be so popular).

Terry: Once a fortnight, and we'll have it on alternate Saturday mornings (There is a stunned silence, then the reaction comes, fast and furious).

Dan: My heart pills!

Ronnie: Never!

Morris: That's the day I go bowling!

Johnny: Now you have really done it. This job of yours has gone to your head. You are not the managing director of this company, you are a supervisor with the title of manager. What makes you think you can change the laid-down working hours of Pinnacle? (He stands and prepares to leave the room) I'm not accepting this; I'm going to see the sales director about it.

Terry: Get back here, Johnny (Johnny keeps going; in three more steps he will be out of the door).Johnny, if you leave this room you are fired (*That* shuts everyone up. Johnny turns, his eyes blazing with anger). Everything I've said here today has been cleared with management, or I wouldn't have said it. I haven't got a swelled head because I suddenly have an office and a title. You are all too smart to think that things could go on as they have been; it had to end some time, and it's no good blaming me because it ended at the same time that I took on this job (He is composed now and is speaking calmly, and the group is listening). As for the job going to my head, not a chance. I have so much to learn that I don't know where to start, and without the help of each one of you I am probably going to fail. Now is our chance to show management what we are made of. If we work together, and believe me, there is nothing I won't do to help you, just as I expect you to help me, we can really–

HOW DID IT GO?

We can leave Terry Sanford and his team of salesmen there. He is just getting into his stride with a get-up-and-at-'em speech and we could almost write his script for him. We wish him well, of course, but how has he done so far, do you think? We are examining the art, not the matter; how he said it, not what he talked about. We are here concerned with his style or philosophy of management.

In other writings of mine – books and articles on my trade of training – I have tried to put on paper words to describe the patterns of management. Whenever I do this I go through dictionary, thesaurus and encyclopaedia, and I find such words as dictatorial, despotic, magisterial and authoritarian on one side and democratic, permissive, participative and representative on the other. I write them all down and then tear up the paper and go back to my two old standbys – Hard and Soft. If you manage people you are a mixture of Hard and Soft management, and your final management style depends on how much of each goes to make up you, the manager. 90 per cent Hard, 10 per cent Soft, and you come across as a shoot-from-the-hip tough guy. 10 per cent Hard, 90 per cent Soft, and the kindly face of a scoutmaster beams out from under the flat hat and above the rows of badges.

In this context, the words Hard and Soft are not terms either of approval or censure; they are merely *descriptions* of management styles. Neither is good nor bad in itself.

Would you like to put a percentage on Terry Sanford's management style during the meeting on which we have just eavesdropped? Without necessarily putting down an exact and arbitrary figure you might feel that he was more Hard than Soft; that he laid it on the line and said: 'That's the way it is,' with little or no opportunity for discussion and no indication that he was prepared to change any of the ideas or procedures he had set out.

This is Hard management; it says, this is what I have decided, so just do it and don't give me a thousand words about it. Soft management would have said: Now, we have a job to do. Here is one way it could be done, but does anyone have a better idea which we can discuss?

Would Terry have done better had he been Softer?

156

Difficult to say, is it not? He might have got the team more quickly to his way of thinking, but then we have the problem of Johnny Farlow, who might have ridden right over Terry had he been Softer, since he may have construed this as a sign of weakness or insecurity.

Let us examine the fascinating stories of Eddie Harderman and Freddie Friendlee. Each of our heroes has just had the wonderful news that he has been promoted from the workforce – production line, service department, internal office staff or field sales force – whatever. He is now a manager; did you hear that, Aunty Flo? A MANAGER! How do they react to this breathtaking event? Eddie Harderman first:

Eddie rushes home and tells his wife: 'I'm an executive!' She, with her mind clearly on the priorities, says: 'Great! We will send the children to private schools, redecorate the house and buy a place on the coast.' Coming down to earth slightly she says: 'I'll phone the rest of the family and tell them the good news.'

Eddie has been sitting and thinking, and some of the initial glow has faded. 'You know,' he says, 'I'm not so sure that it *is* good news. I have never managed anybody before. Now I have six people under me, and I don't know if I will be able to get *on* with them.'

Now, because women tend to be a little Harder rather than Softer in management, perhaps his wife says: 'What do you mean, get on with them? Eddie, get it into your head that you are the *boss* now. The team has to get on with *you*!' She goes out to do a little bragging around the neighbourhood about her bigshot husband, leaving Eddie to pursue a new and compelling train of thought. 'She's right, as usual,' he thinks. 'Those guys had better toe the line or they won't know what's hit them!' He develops this theme in his mind until by the time he gets to work next day we have a pocket-sized Abdul the Damned on our hands.

His workforce quickly realises that Eddie has decided to take the Hard Road. His people go along with this (it is inconvenient to resign just at the moment), but Eddie has not understood something about the way that groups work, and this could lead to his downfall. Before he was promoted the group looked like this:

Now it looks like this:

Now, a group is a self-healing entity; it closes itself up when a part is taken from it, just as an insect which has lost a leg will carry on quite happily without it, and the wound will heal without any function impaired. In Eddie's case the group will do precisely that:

E

The members of the team, faced with Hard management from someone who a few short weeks ago was merely one of the bunch, will apparently submit to Eddie's tough line, but in fact they are watching him very carefully. They are waiting for him to make his first managerial mistake (which he will do quite soon, since he is new at the job) and the moment he makes that mistake they will crucify him – and they will do it *as a group*.

To an outsider, one who knows nothing about the subtleties of management, it must seem that when someone is placed in a position of authority over others, that person has all the clout, all the muscle, all the ammunition in any confrontation and that the subordinates to that person have none. Nothing, of course, can be further from the truth. The truth is that if for some reason you don't like your manager, if something about your relationship with him gives rise to frustration, resentment, envy or anger, then you often have very powerful weapons to bring into the arena of your working environment. You can produce a situation which all managers fear. They may not know it by the name I give it, but they are aware of it and they are constantly on the lookout for it. I call it Destructive Compliance, and it goes like this. I work for you and I hate your guts. You give me an instruction. I carry out the instruction to the letter, exactly and precisely the way you told me to do it. The result is a disaster, and the one left holding the damp baby is you. You see, I have spent some time working out how to carry out the instruction so that it will blow up in your face, and I do it without disobeying you in any way. It is called Dumb Insolence in the army, and there it's a crime.

So Eddie Harderman, by emulating some of the less attractive characteristics of our twentieth-century despots, lays himself open to problems which could keep him staring at the ceiling all night.

What about Freddie?

Freddy Friendlee has an absolute horror of 'putting on the dog' in his new found elevation. His first act

after getting over the hangover consequent to his cele-
bratory party is to call a meeting of his team. His team,
who have always thought of Freddie as an amiable
clown, are still a little shaken at the news, and when
they file into the meeting room they look at Freddie
with the expressions of people who have just seen a
horse climb a ladder; they can't believe the evidence of
their senses.

Freddie stands up at the head of the conference
table and spreads his hands in a gesture of wonder-
ment. 'Hey, chaps,' he says with a big grin. 'So they
made me the manager. Isn't that crazy?'

'That's crazy, all right,' says the group. On that
point at least there is no disagreement.

'Now, look,' says Freddie. 'I want you all to know
one thing. Sure, I'm the manager, but nothing has
really *changed*. We are still the same happy band of
buddies we were before, right? I mean, okay, I have
responsibilities and duties which I didn't have before,
and if anybody here has any problems, well, I'll be
happy to do what I can to help, but for the rest why,
we are still *friends*, right?'

'Of course; sure; don't you worry, Freddie; things
will go on just as they did before.' The group is quick
to assure Freddie that he is right and that nothing has
changed. That is what the group *says*, but while Freddie
may hope that the pleasant relationships he has been
used to are still there, the group knows differently. The
group has an animal awareness that Freddie can keep
calling them his 'buddies' but the truth is that they are
no longer his buddies or, rather, he is no longer theirs.
Freddie is now Fuzz, he is Establishment, and he has
lost for ever his position in the team which he valued
so much.

Freddie doesn't understand this but his erstwhile

mates certainly do. However, why bother to try to disillusion Freddie? Why make waves? We have La Dolce Vita going here, men, with a boss who doesn't act like a boss. Relax and enjoy it – while it lasts.

It doesn't last, of course; how could it? One day Freddie wakes up to the realisation that there is a crisis of some sort facing his little unit, and immediate action is required. He calls the boys together. 'All right, this is it,' he says. 'We are going to have to pull out all the stops on this one. Let's go.' The reaction of his 'buddies' to this call to arms is quite horrifying to Freddie:

'What's your hurry, Freddie? Let's all have another cup of coffee before we do anything drastic.'

'I don't think that's our problem; let someone else do it.'

'Count me out, Freddie. This is my afternoon for jogging.'

'I'm going to take a couple of days off. I don't feel so good.'

'Freddie, if you are so keen to have it done, why don't you do it yourself?'

Incredulous that his chums would even think of not supporting him now that he really needs them, Freddie says: 'Come *on*, now, fellows, this is an emergency! Let's get *going!*'

'Don't get your knickers in a knot, mate.'

'What happened to that bull about us being all pals together, Freddie?'

'Shut up, Freddie, will you, I've got a headache.'

- And Freddie realises to his horror that you can't be everyone's pal one minute and then, when it suits you, don the mantle of authority, and expect people to accept you in both rôles.

161

Eddie was wrong in deciding to be Hard, Hard, Hard; Freddie was wrong in deciding to be Soft, Soft, Soft. As is so often the case with anything new, both of these new managers swung over to extremes. Does this mean that the ideal is always fifty/fifty, Hard/Soft? By no means; if that were true there would be little reason to record most of the cases in this book. Many times do we have to move, sometimes quite strongly, towards Hard or towards Soft management as the occasion requires it. To take one instance only: many managers seem to believe that when handling a brand-new group of employees, the softer the management style the better. This they feel will let the new people in at the shallow end, will temper the wind. This is a wrong philosophy. The truth is that the new person looks for strong, sure, expert leadership in these strange and even frightening surroundings. He does not want to be asked his opinion of what is best to do, he wants to be told exactly what is required of him, and he wants to be watched to see that he does it right. Much later, when he has found his feet, he will no doubt appreciate it when his manager shows his faith in him enough to let him make some small decisions on his own and use his own initiative, *but not yet*.

Harder first, Softer later, is a very sound management rule.

In the cases of Eddie and Freddie we know that neither showed very much management expertise, but oddly enough it was Freddie who got himself into a virtually irretrievable position with his 'Soft first, Hard when you have to' style. Although Eddie was wrong to show the iron fist from the very beginning, it is unlikely that he would get into quite the mess that Freddie found himself in.

It is always interesting for me in my management

Clinics to see, when I give the delegates a case study to ponder over, how often it is the new managers who come out confidently with a solution while the experienced managers scratch their heads. In most cases, the solutions produced by the new boys or girls are a swing of the pendulum to one extreme or the other; very Hard or very Soft. It is the experienced managers who, when they do venture an opinion, usually choose a much less radical solution.

In the old fighter planes there was a 'gate' on the throttle control. When you *really* had to you could push the throttle through this gate and it would give you the extra power you needed to get yourself out of a bad jam. It was an extreme step, though, and every pilot knew that it was for emergency *only*. So is it with Very Hard or Very Soft; only when you *have* to.

13

The fall of the house of Isher

Frank Isher is a branch manager of Tiger TV and HiFi, and right at this moment he is wishing that he had taken holy orders or become an Arctic explorer – anything other than being a branch manager for Tiger TV and HiFi. Three pieces of bad news have hit him on the same morning, all serious and all unexpected.

Item: The Travellers Joy, a hotel with forty-five TV sets has telephoned to cancel their maintenance contract because, they say, of unsatisfactory work by Lofty Homer, Tiger's branch service man.

Item: The company sales figures have come out and Frank's branch is by far the lowest, which means that Harry Landers the branch salesman has been falling down on the job.

Item: Mr Owen Ferry, a long-time customer of the branch, has just barged into Frank's office waving a bunch of accounts, statements, delivery slips and credit notes which he says are a lot of rubbish. 'Mistakes on every one of them, dammit! Can't you get your paperwork straightened out, Isher?' Wendy Walton is the branch receptionist, bookeeper, typist and filing clerk, so something is badly wrong in her department.

Frank has decided, rightly or wrongly, to handle all three problems together, and he has told his entire staff, consisting of Lofty Homer, Harry Landers and Wendy Walton, that there will be a meeting in his office right after the doors close at five tonight. His manner as he handed out this piece of information was such that any complaint about the overtime was stilled at birth. It is now five o'clock and all four of them are in Frank's office.

WHAT DO YOU THINK?

Is this a good idea, to try to solve all three problems at one meeting? You might say that it depends on the cause of the problems, and that if anything embarrassing about Lofty, Harry or Wendy is likely to come out then it is not a good idea. On the other hand if the problems are such that they are soluble in a sort of team effort then, yes, it could be a good thing to have them all together; it might even improve morale in the little group. Well, for better or worse, Frank is now committed to a group meeting.

Frank (he is determined not to lose his temper, at least until he discovers what is going on): When I came into the office this morning I felt as though the roof had suddenly fallen on my head. I got three pieces of information that I could have done without. First, the Travellers Joy phoned to cancel their contract, which means that we have lost the most valuable single maintenance contract on our books. Second–

Lofty: that wasn't my fault. I–

Frank (Firmly): No, Lofty. You will get your chance later. Second, the overall sales figures landed on my desk and this branch is dead bottom of the list, and the computer print-out has a special love-letter written across it in Mr Waterson's own handwriting; it says: 'Not good enough, Frank!' Which of course makes me feel–

Harry: The figures don't tell the whole story–

Frank (Even more firmly): Not now, Harry. Later. - Which of course makes me feel just fine. Third, Mr Owen Ferry stormed into this office and nearly drowned me in a sea of paper. He says his accounts with us are a mess, and looking through what he chucked on my desk I'd say that 'mess' doesn't even begin to describe it. Now, something–

Wendy: I'm sorry about Mr Ferry's accounts, but–

Frank (Very, very firmly): Wendy! You will all get a chance to talk in a moment. Now, something is very seriously wrong in this branch and I must tell you that I am flabbergasted. I hired each one of you when I was sent here to open this branch. I selected you myself, and trained you and supervised you until you got the hang of the jobs. How does it happen that each one of you has failed in one of the most important aspects of his or her job? Lofty, the Travellers says your work is unsatisfactory. Harry, the computer says *your* work is unsatisfactory. Wendy, Mr Ferry says *your* work is unsatisfactory. What the hell is going on? (All three start talking at once) All right! One at a time. Lofty, you first, and remember all of you that I want explanations and not excuses.

166

Lofty (With righteous indignation): That silly fat sod of a room manager at the Travellers is a bloody liar when he says my work is unsatisfactory. I personally checked with the porter's desk yesterday – all TV complaints come to the head porter – and he told me that every set was working perfectly!

Frank: Is that really so?

Lofty: Why don't you phone him right now and see for yourself?

Frank: Do you know, I think I will (He does just that and speaks to the head porter himself). He says that every set is working and that when you fix a set it stays fixed.

Lofty (Triumphantly): See? See? What's unsatisfactory about that?

Frank (Slowly): Nothing at all; it's very good (Lofty smiles complacently). So tell me, why have we lost the contract?

Lofty (Stops smiling): Oh, that stupid bastard of a floor manager was against me from the start. He has always had his knife into me, always looking for an excuse to chuck us out!

Frank: And what – excuse did he find, Lofty?

Lofty (Defensively): Oh, nothing. Nothing at all, really.

Frank: You were keen for me to phone the head porter. Shall I also phone the floor manager?

Lofty: No! He – he's busy round this time of day. He won't thank you for disturbing him.

Frank: Lofty, you will now tell me exactly what

happened at the Travellers. I am going to check with them anyway, so your story had better be the truth, the whole truth, and nothing but the truth, so help you.

Lofty: Look Frank, it was just a couple of silly little things (Frank is the Sphinx). Well, there was a call that the set in room 406 had lost the picture and the bloke wanted to see the football. So I got the number wrong and banged on the door of 604 – it was a mistake anyone could have made. Got a honeymoon couple out of bed. Well, I told them I had to check the set and I checked the set. Silly female ran into the bathroom crying and the bloke made a fuss with the management (Looks at Frank but Frank is carved out of ice). So, I'm fixing the set in the residents' lounge and this old fool totters past and puts his bloody great foot down on a printed circuit. Well, of course, I told him to watch it (Hesitates). Well, so I said to him, hey, get your eyes out of your – dammit, that was an expensive part! (He looks at Frank but Frank is looking at nothing at all) That's all, Frank. Oh, well, that damned floor manager thinks that a man can work with his hands and still look like a tailor's dummy. I tell you, he is always picking on me, and yesterday I – well, I told him that I – (He stops). Well, I told him.

(There is a thoughtful silence.)

Frank: I see. So the floor manager has his knife into you? I can't see why. After all, you didn't do anything except humiliate a bride on her honeymoon, strew your gear all over the floor and insult a guest when he walks past, walk into a high-class hotel dressed as though you live under a bridge, and then when all this is pointed out to you, you tell a valuable customer where to go. But that's all right, because the TV sets are all working (Lofty leans forward). Not a word, Lofty; not a single syllable. I'll get back to you in a moment. Harry: your sales figures are not only 'not good enough' as Mr Waterson put it, they are plain rotten. They could cost me my job, and while that may not lose you any sleep, my boy, they could also cost you *your* job. Talk!

Harry (Plaintively): Gee, Frank, you know I work a full day. You get my call reports, you have been out with me, you see me telephoning, getting the appointments, calling back. I don't know what else I can do.

Frank: I'm not saying you don't work hard, Harry. I know you aren't spinning your wheels. I must tell you that you worry me because I can't see what is wrong. You know the product range; I have never asked you a question about the products that you have not been able to answer. You seem to get on reasonably well with the customers, too. What is it?

Harry (Miserable): Beats me.

Frank: Let's see; you came to us from that Kwiksell crowd, didn't you? What did you sell there? I've forgotten what you told me.

Harry: Gee, Frank, just about everything. Razor blades, batteries for cassette recorders, sticky tape, roller ball pens – you name it, I sold it.

Frank: Those were *impulse* items. Who were your customers? Chain stores, Supermarkets, like that?

Harry (Animated now): That's right! You see, you

have these display stands at the checkout counters, and when the customers come through–

Frank: Thank you for the lecture, Harry; I know about impulse buying. Where were you before Kwiksell?

Harry: With the D'lishush Company; you know, sweets and chocolates; remember, it was on my application form when you hired me.

Frank: And you came from a background of fast-moving consumer items straight into the appliance business. Why? Why did you apply for this job?

Harry: Well, Frank, it was a chance to make a lot more than I was earning. At my two previous companies I was on a straight salary; here I get salary and commission, except (his face falls), except–

Frank: Except that with your lousy sales volume there has been damned little commission.

Harry (With feeling): *Damned* little.

Frank (Sighs): I'll get back to you, too. Now, Wendy; what is the problem with Mr Ferry's accounts?

Wendy (Busily tearing a handkerchief to pieces with nervous fingers): I'm sorry, Mr Isher–

Frank: Wendy, I've told you before, in this office we are on first-name terms.

Wendy: I'm sorry, Frank. I must have messed them up. I really tried to get it right this time, but the discounts always confuse me.

Frank: Wendy, have you been adding the discounts together again? How many times have I told you that when the discount structure is less 12½ per cent, less

7½ per cent, that it is *not* the same as less 20 per cent? (Wendy carefully examines her ruined hankie) You are a real asset to this office, Wendy. You get on well with all the customers, your telephone manner is excellent, your typing and filing are perfect. Why can't you improve on your bookkeeping? Heavens, girl, it's so elementary it isn't even bookkeeping, really.

Wendy: I *know*. I'm not good with figures. I told you when I came here that I had never done any figurework, but you said it was so simple that any idiot could do it (She puts her face into her hands). I must be worse than an idiot!

Frank: But I've shown you time and time again how to do the accounts. It's all so easy! (Wendy shakes her head vigorously, her face still hidden behind her hands) Well?

Wendy (She moves a finger away from her face, revealing one accusing eye.) You don't really teach me how to do it, Frank. You just do it yourself and say: 'There you are, that's how it's done,' and walk away. I see you doing it but I still don't see how *I* should do it. I'm *not* stupid!

(Frank sits back and surveys his team. He has the feeling that his branch is falling down about his ears. He looks at each of them in turn: Lofty, Harry, Wendy.)

Frank: What the hell am I to do with you people? I have a serviceman who is anti-social, a salesman who shouldn't be in this industry at all and a clerk who doesn't know the twelve times table. What do I do now – fire the lot of you and start all over again?

WHAT DO YOU THINK?

It seems that Frank Isher is justified in feeling hard done by; his team has let him down in all departments. Should he fire them all and hire another serviceman, salesman and clerk? Suppose you were Mr Waterson, Frank's boss in head office, and just suppose that you had had a bug in Frank's office so that you could have listened in to that unhappy meeting; would you have suggested to Frank that, yes, it is best to cut your losses, get shot of all three of his washouts and start from scratch?

We don't know what Mr Waterson would have suggested about Frank Isher's staff. What we do know if we have really examined the situation is that if he really had been listening in, and if he were really on top of his job, he would immediately have fired Frank Isher.

'That's not fair!' I hear the protest from a thousand throats. 'Just because Frank happens to have three no-hopers on his hands is no reason to fire him!'

No? Come back with me to re-examine the situation, and let us start with Harry, our non-selling salesman. Harry applied for a job with Tiger TV and HiFi for one reason and one only – to earn more money than he had ever earned before. Nothing against that, you say; the man is ambitious, he wants to better his financial situation. Nothing against it indeed, except that Frank did not go into this reason when he took Harry on. He should have picked up the clues which would have shown him that not only had Harry had no experience in selling electrical equipment (which would not by itself have been an automatic turn-down) but that Harry actually had no interest in and no aptitude for selling this type of product. We saw a glimpse

172

of it, didn't we? When Harry was talking about his two previous jobs it showed that he really was interested in the fast-moving type of impulse products such as razor-blades and sweets.

Harry applied for a job which he had no chance of succeeding in. That was not very smart of him but it was perhaps a natural thing for him to do. What was unforgiveable was that Frank hired him without digging into his experience, his preference and his aptitude.

That was stupid.

Wendy Walton seems to be unusually scatter-brained about figures. Apparently even the most simple credit notes, invoices and delivery slips are beyond her grasp. Surely that isn't Frank Isher's fault? She was hired mainly for her typing, filing and general office work, and this she does excellently. The bookkeeping is a fairly small part of her job, and surely one would have the right to assume that she could pick up the basics as she went along?

But has Frank taught her anything at all? We quote Wendy: 'You don't really *teach* me how to do it. You just do it yourself and say: "There you are, that's how it's done," and walk away. I see you doing it but I still don't see how *I* should do it. I'm *not* stupid!'

She is *not* stupid. Frank said himself that she was an asset to the office, that her other work was perfect. Frank did not teach her the job at all; he seemed to feel that she would absorb it through the skin by osmosis, merely by watching him do a few examples.

That was stupid.

Lofty Homer sounds like the worst problem of the three. Here is the classic case of the worker who, while he is technically competent, has no idea of how to handle people, so he does the job perfectly and then mucks the whole thing up by antagonising the customer.

Is this another case of Frank hiring the wrong person? Not really. You hire a technician first and foremost for his technical abilities, and seldom if ever do you look really deeply into his people skills. Is it a fault in training, then? Hardly; can you see Frank running a one-man course for Lofty in Customer Relations?

No. Here, Frank should have checked on Lofty's performance in the customers' premises. In a larger branch this would have been the job of the foreman or supervisor, who would be in charge of several technicians, but here it was clearly Frank's job. He should have made random calls, both by telephone and in person, to see that customers were satisfied with every aspect of Lofty's work, which would have included his appearance, manners and attitude. Lofty was not to blame. He thought of his job as fixing TV sets, not acting as a public relations officer for Tiger TV and HiFi. Frank should have recognised Lofty's strengths on the technical side and his weaknesses on the people side; he should have made some calls with him and pointed out the pitfalls of bad customer relations while actually on the job with Lofty. Instead he seemed to expect that Lofty Homer would somehow combine the technical expertise of Thomas Edison with the personality of Billy Graham.

That was stupid.

WHAT HAVE WE GOT HERE?

What we have is the fall of the house of Frank Isher, brought about because of three fundamental weaknesses in his management of people:

With Harry he did not hire correctly.
With Wendy he did not train correctly.
With Lofty he did not supervise correctly.

Selection, Training, Supervision – the absolute corner-stones of good management. These are the true basics. Without them nothing in management is possible.

But what about Motivation – surely that is a basic? By no means; motivation is far up the scale of sophisticated management. It is the roof and spire of our building, but roofs and spires don't stand on air, they stand on solid foundations, and in good management the solid foundations are Selection, Training, Supervision.

Get the right people, train them properly, supervise them effectively – and all things are possible.

14

What is happening at the coal-face?

In the previous section we examined the case of Frank Isher and we found that he had been guilty of three basic sins of omission. Is Frank's case widespread and endemic, or is it so rare that it is not worth bothering about? Let us see, shall we? Let us look at some examples, and may a thunderbolt from heaven strike me dead if a single example of those which follow is a lie; every one actually happened, so help me.

Consider for starters the enormous sums of money spent by the financial houses – banks, investment corporations, building societies and the like – in advertising their expertise in making your money grow, in providing a secure retirement, in making you rich. What they are doing of course is trying to get you and me to dig under the mattress, pull out the old rugby stocking which is our bank, fish out our few bucks, and take it in to their place of business where they will instantly invest it so that we get maximum return while paying minimum income tax on it. Truly, they spend millions every year on advertising, merchandising, and otherwise promoting themselves. 'Come in and talk to us!' they say. 'We are the friendly experts. We are waiting to serve you!'

All right, suppose that you decide: 'Gee, they sound like nice people. I think I'll take my modest pile of dough in and see what they say.'

So you do. You walk into this impressive banking hall, all marble pillars, plate glass and heavy carpeting. You go up to the counter.

Now it is time for me to introduce you to Dimples. She is the one standing behind that counter. She is the one with the friendly smile and the financial expertise you have seen in the TV advertisements for this financial institution. What about Dimples? Well, she is nineteen years old, her shoes are too tight, she has just been warned by her boss for taking too long over her coffee-break, she has low-back pain, and in view of what happened last night she is hoping to God that the Pill is as reliable as they say.

What are your chances with Dimples? Is she really going to give you that helpful, smiling, expert advice that they claim?

More? Cast your eye over the promotional material for the car-rental companies which crosses your desk every week and which assures you of the fantastic care they take of their cars and their customers. I picked up a car at an airport from one of the major car-hire companies (no, not the one you are thinking of, the other one) and headed towards my destination and, as it turned out, near-death. When a cow tried to commit suicide in front of the car and I stamped on the brake in the middle of a shower of rain the car immediately slewed round and tried to exceed the speed-limit in reverse. Nigel Mansell would have fainted, but I managed to save both the cow and myself from whatever after-life our respective virtues and sins entitled us to. The attendant at the service station where I had the tyres checked couldn't believe the gauge – left front tyre, 13 pounds per square inch; right front tyre, 37.

One more? A wealthy friend of mine went into a car showroom to make enquiries about a state-of-the-art luxury car (which he could have bought with the walking-around money in his wallet). The salesroom person (I refuse to dignify him with the title of 'salesman') looked him over and said: 'Buddy, we don't give test drives to just anybody, you know.'

Just what the hell is happening out there? This is being written when we are in the worst economic mess that the world has been in since 1929, with millions unemployed and scores of companies going bankrupt every single day, and when I take back a roller ball refill that won't work I am asked: 'Are you sure that this isn't an old one that you have used up?' This is accompanied by a look that says she saw my picture in the police station.

Now, the scary thing is not merely that all this has happened to me or my friends and family in recent weeks. What is really frightening is that every one of you who is reading this can cap my stories with at least one of your own ('What is Beer crying about? He should have been around when they had to come back four times before my new shower door would close properly!').

The people concerned here are those who deal directly with the customer. In business jargon they are the ones 'At the sharp end' or 'Working the coal-face'. They are the counter-girls, the technicians, the receptionists, the salespeople, the maintenance men, the order clerks, the switchboard people.

When I am in the process of setting up a series of

training clinics for a client company I try to get 'inside' the company as far as possible, to get a feel of its 'peopleness', as it were. I often sit in on top-level discussions with senior people and I often hear them say something like: 'The people at the sharp end are the most important people in our company. We are a *people* organisation.'

–And often, this is one big lie.

Now it may seem that from the horrible examples I have given I am blaming Dimples (one of that company's 'investment counsellors', Lord help us all), or the man who put the air in my tyres, or the car showroom inhabitant who saw through my millionaire friend for the chancer he obviously was, or the girl in the stationery shop who recognised my criminal tendencies. I am not. I truly am not pointing a finger at any of these people. The whole point of this section is that when you and I get indifferent service or performance we tend to blame the people at the counter or grease-bay or telephone. *They are not the problem.* They are a symptom of the sickness, not its cause. The cause, the real problem, is one of *attitude*, and it is further up the ladder; in most cases, very much further up.

I recently ran a series of sales and management clinics for a national chain. At the end of the series I was asked to give my impressions of company strategy in general – anything which may have struck me during my stint with the company's people. I am not a management consultant and I hesitated, but the chief executive officer pressed me to speak. 'Say anything you like,' he said. 'Don't pull any punches.'

'All right,' I said. 'Your main problem is that you don't pay your counter staff enough.'

Well, I couldn't have been more unpopular if I had suggested that the managing director should stop flashing in the typists' pool. I was coldly informed that I had to be wrong, since the company never had any difficulty getting applicants for jobs behind the counters; ergo, their salary levels were fair and even generous. I saw no benefit to anyone, especially me, in quoting what one of their departmental managers had said to me: 'I am allowed to pay about three-quarters of the going rate,' she said, and she was nearly in tears in frustration. 'Of *course* we get applicants for jobs; jobs are scarce and people need the work. But who do you think apply for jobs with us? I'll tell you: the cast-offs, the losers, the second-rate!'

It is an interesting exercise to ponder on the ratiocination of a company which will spend millions on advertising to bring people into its place of business, where they will encounter staff who seem to have been hired to chase them out again.

The truth is that in most companies, in most industries, the 'coal-face' is being wrongly worked; the 'sharp end' is no longer sharp. In the previous section Frank Isher had three people who for all the good they were doing for the company might have been working for the opposition.

Very well, what exactly is wrong and what can be done to put it right? I have said that the problem is one of attitude of management, but that is too broad an indictment to help us much. Let us postulate a correct attitude for management; they want to do the right things, they simply don't know what these right things are. What can they do?

What they can do comes under the three basics we mentioned in the case of the fall of the house of Frank Isher: Selection, Training, Supervision. Let us examine each one of these and see how they fit into the solution to the problem.

GET THE RIGHT PEOPLE

I know nothing of gardening, but I am told that you can water, fertilise, harrow, mulch and prune yourself to a standstill, but unless the seed you plant in the beginning is first-class you are wasting your time. The analogy is exact: you can train, teach, supervise, motivate, appraise and delegate yourself into an oxygen tent, but unless you get the right people to start with you are wasting your time. If you had to choose one management skill only in order to have a good team working for you then it would have to be Staff Selection. Hire a good person and all the other skills such as training will make him better; hire a lemon and training will only make him a trained lemon.

As to how to go about selection and recruitment of staff, if you are not entirely happy with your own efforts in this direction then perhaps it is time to hand the job over to the professionals. If you do decide to use the specialised outfits who advertise, interview, evaluate and use all the mystiques of selection then the only way to do it is to give them every single piece of information about the job that you can. By all means produce a full job specification, and not only the job itself should be studied but also your company; where do you sit in the industry? Are you a growth company? Do you promote from within wherever possible? And so on. The more you tell them the closer they can get to helping you get the right people for that specific job.

And if you have the slightest feeling that your pay scales are not right for the job or the industry, there are even consultants who will tell you what you should be paying your staff in every one of the departments in your company. A chat with one of these organisations could be a traumatic experience for the executives of some of the companies who believe that they are 'people-oriented'.

MAKE GOOD PEOPLE BETTER

This section is not a thinly-disguised commercial for Michael Beer Training Clinics because the training we are discussing here can best be done by your own people within your own company, since it is a continuous, long-term process; outside training (or at least, training in your company by an outsider)is generally 'crash' type training – short-duration, intensive, specific. This has its place, of course, but it is largely useless unless it is closely tied in with the company's long-term development programme.

The problem with training is the myth that it has already been done. If we were to investigate each one of the horrible examples in the beginning of this section *we would find that everyone of them had been 'trained'*. Ask their managers: 'Oh, yes; Felix? Beverley? Betty? Mark? Yes, they have been through all our training courses. They are all fully-trained.' Well, the training, unlike their vaccination, didn't take, did it? It didn't take because they are *not* fully trained. *Nobody is ever fully-trained*. We can't drag people through a few days in a training room and then with a sigh of satisfaction throw them in at the deep end. Training is not a cholera shot which you get before you travel to Hong Kong and which lasts three years before you need a booster shot. It is a never-ending process in which every single member of the staff, from the very bottom to the very top, is involved.

SEE THAT THEY STAY GOOD

A manager once said to me: 'I run my team on a very long leash. I don't breathe down their necks every moment of the day. I trust them to do the job of work that I hired them to do, and they know that if they have any problems at all, that my door is always open.'

Now, doesn't that sound good? Here is a manager who treats his people like adults. He doesn't insult them by watching their every move as though they were irresponsible teenagers. Surely his team will react to this attitude by acting in a responsible and adult way! Maybe, but when the time came for me to work with this team I found that they had problems which the manager had not even dreamed of. The biggest problem of all came out not in the Clinic but when I was having a drink with two of the delegates after hours. One of the best participators of the day said, talking about his manager: 'Joe is a pleasant enough chap, all right, but he doesn't really give a damn about what we are *doing*.'

I'll tell you something which you may not believe. You may reject this piece of information because you have heard of people resenting it when their managers 'breathe down their necks'. All very well, but do you know that for every complaint I hear about over-close supervision, I hear five complaints that: 'My manager doesn't even know what I *do* every day!' – And the obvious corollary is that he doesn't *care*.

Supervision does not imply a lack of trust by the manager in his workforce. Supervision does not mean suspiciously watching every move your workers make because you are convinced that they are all loafers, thieves, or opposition spies. To a good manager supervision means assessing abilities, performances and attitudes, and guiding and counselling, and correcting weaknesses and reinforcing strengths.

Perhaps it is time for all managers at whatever level to take a long, hard look at that part of their companies where the physical work is being done. Is the coal-face really being properly worked? Is the sharp end still really sharp? If it is not then let us quit blaming the clerk, the artisan, the operator and the repairman and examine very closely our own performance as managers.

Especially let us go back to the basics – the three pillars of wisdom – Selection, Training, Supervision. Lose sight of only one of these and not all the advertising, merchandising, promotions or public relations in the world will compensate; get all three of them right and suddenly so many things lock sweetly into place.

15

Who should get the job?

You are the Sales Director of an office appliance company which has recently obtained the sole agency for a new office copier. While this machine is slightly higher in price than competitive copiers it does have several features which make it particularly useful for professional people such as doctors, dentists and lawyers. You need a salesperson to put the machine on the market in the central city area, and a short list of five applicants has been compiled by the five people in your company who are usually involved with the hiring of sales staff (Not that it matters, but they happen to be the Personnel Manager, the Assistant Sales Director, The Training Manager, the City Branch Manager and the Copier Division Manager).

Each one of these people has a favourite in the short list, and wouldn't you know it, each one is different. You have called a meeting of the five so that each one can put the case for his choice; at the same time, since each one hates the choices of the other four, you will be hearing both the points for and against each applicant. Also, since all selection interviews in your company are taped, you will hear a quote from each applicant.

It is up to you to choose the best of the five. Please note that this is a case history; it happened, and one of the applicants was chosen. At the bottom of an appraisal form on the successful applicant one year later, you scribbled: 'It seems that we made a *reasonable* choice.'

Here we go.

The proposer of ANDY ABBOTT says:

I like this applicant. He is twenty-three years old, passed his A-levels well, spent a year at university doing analytical chemistry and left to get into the excitement of commercial life. He spent six months as a sales trainee with an oil company but found the work dull. After that he had two years as a salesman for a manufacturer's representative – that's a good grounding for any salesman – where he specialised in tools and hardware. He has just returned from a hiking holiday on the Continent, which means that he has already sown his wild oats. He is very presentable, he speaks well – highly articulate chap, this – clearly intelligent.

ANDY ABBOTT'S QUOTE:

'I am ready to settle down and this is the sort of company I should like to be associated with. I know nothing about copiers but I learn quickly and I expect no trouble in getting to know the product. My father is a doctor, and I believe that I can sell to this type of prospect. I look on selling as a means to prove myself

186

worthy of an executive position when I have gained the experience.'

Comments from the other managers:

'Not a chance. Hire him and he'll be off on another hiking holiday within a year.'
'Why did he drop out of university?'
'He thinks that he will be able to sell to his father's friends, and it won't work.'
'He is twenty-three years old and already he is talking about an executive position in the company!'

The proposer of BILL BENSON says:

Now, this is a really solid citizen. He is forty-one years old and, except for three years as a toolmaker after he left school, his whole life has been spent in selling. He has had only four jobs in all – five years with a milling company, nine years in canned foods, and (his present job) four years selling the Eezee-fax copier, which as you all know is a cheaper machine than ours. He has therefore had experience of our industry. He is neat in appearance, he speaks slowly and carefully, even if not very fluently. He is married with three sons.

BILL BENSON'S QUOTE

'I am sure that I can put this machine on the market. I have had plenty of experience of selling copiers and I know all the makes and their good and bad points. As far as I can see from a first look at it, this is a good machine – it's got things which none of the others have. If we can get over the price problem we should be able to hit the opposition hard.'

Comments from the other managers:

'At forty-one he is too old. You can't teach an old dog new tricks.'
'He hasn't really had a very exciting career path, has he? Still a salesman after all that time in selling.'
'He has a negative attitude about the price of the product; when he can't sell it he will come crying for a price reduction.'
'Won't professional people get impatient with his slow, careful way of speaking?'

The proposer of CHARLIE CASE says:

You should hear this man talk; he is a convincing speaker. He is twenty-nine years old and he was a bank-clerk for six years. Then he began selling cars and he is still doing that. He is married, no children. He took a correspondence course in Marketing and passed the first year. He failed the second year but he intends to finish the course in time. He is fairly presentable, perhaps a little casual in his dress but we can always fix that. He limps badly at the moment, from a car accident last year. He is a good-looking guy.

CHARLIE CASE'S QUOTE

'I like selling and intend to make it my career, but car selling is not for me. I would like to sell a quality article, as I believe that quality can always overrule the price objection. I am mechanically minded and I will have no difficulty in understanding the technical points of the machine.'

Comments from the other managers:

188

'From bank clerk to car salesman? Now copiers? This man doesn't know what he wants.'

'He sounds slap-dash to me – and whose fault was that car accident? I'd want to investigate that.'

'If he believes that quality can always overrule the price objection then he probably still believes in the tooth fairy.'

'He's not a stick-at-it character; he will never finish that course in Marketing.'

The proposer of DAWN DRAKE says:

The best of the bunch. She is thirty-three years old and has an Arts degree. She worked in her uncle's business as a clerk until he died, then as organising secretary for an important branch office of a political party. While doing this she read books on selling and actually took an evening course in salesmanship. She dresses stylishly, speaks extremely well. She is divorced, no children. She could deal at any level of customer.

DAWN DRAKE'S QUOTE

'I have waited for some time before deciding on a selling career, and have prepared myself for the job. I like the concept of persuading people to buy through a logical and convincing sales presentation. I have done a good deal of public speaking during my time in politics, and while this is naturally different from a sales talk, at least it means that I should have no fear of nervousness when talking to prospective buyers.'

Comments from the other managers:

'Sorry; this job is too tough for a woman.' (This got a

glare from the Personnel Manager, who did not as it happens have Dawn Drake as her favourite but who nevertheless didn't appreciate the male chauvinistic attitude.)

'She hasn't ever done any selling. In spite of her taking a selling course and reading the selling books, the risk is too high.'

'I don't like the political background; she is going to lecture to people, not sell to them.'

'Why did she spend all that time working for her uncle and only stop when he died? Was she hiding from the competitive world outside?'

The proposer of EDDIE EATON says:

This is a very likeable person; I was immediately attracted to him. He is twenty-seven years old, passed his O-levels and became an apprentice mechanic. Most of his working life has been mechanical, but three years ago he became a life insurance agent and he has really done well in this line which, as you all know, is not an easy selling job. He now wants to join a company in a steady job. He is taking elocution lessons off his own bat to improve his speech, which I admit is a little rough. He is presentable and dresses well, though of course his hands show his working background. He is married with one baby daughter.

EDDIE EATON'S QUOTE

'I am ambitious to improve myself, to give my family the things I didn't have as a child. This machine looks like the answer to copying needs, and although I can't say for sure that I will be able to sell it, I am ready to give it a good go. So long as the company is prepared to back me up with good after-sales service, I will be confident about offering the machine to prospects.'

Comments from the other managers:

'He sounds all right but the truth is that he is too much of a rough diamond for the type of buyer we are looking at.'
'He doesn't seem sure of himself – he says he will give it a 'good go'; we need more than that.'
'Why is he leaving life insurance if he is doing well at it? Successful life agents earn good money, and I don't buy this excuse of wanting a steady job.'
'Why has he still got rough hands after three years away from the bench? Is he still working on cars in his back yard? We don't need a part-time mechanic, we need a full-time salesman.'

Well, there are your five applicants, Mr Sales Director; how do you like them? In addition to what your managers have said both for and against them, your keen, perceptive mind will of course have picked up other points and questions, and some of these, in no particular order of importance, are below:

    –Andy Abbott may not be as lacking in direction as it seems; he seems to have initiative and to be prepared to look around until he finds the job which really suits him.

    –Bill Benson may indeed not have had an exciting career up to now, but do you really need someone to fill your chair? Are you not simply looking for a dependable salesman?

    –Charlie Case can't be faulted for being a bank clerk; many boys are thrust into that sort of job because their fathers consider it a 'safe' way of life. Perhaps the fact that he broke away from it is in his favour?

–Dawn Drake is much too intelligent to spout at her prospects as though she were addressing a political meeting. Wouldn't the fact that she is a woman be in her favour, making it easier for her to get an interview?

–Eddie Eaton is the only one of the five who sees how important it is to have good after-sales backup; that's a realistic approach.

–And so on. What is happening here is an *evaluation* of these people, and it is something that a manager does every day of his working life. Not that he hires people every day, but he lives and works with his present staff every day, and every day he is feeding on-the-spot evaluations of them into his mental computer. The metaphor is appropriate; just as the computer is a binary instrument, working on a go/no-go system, so does a manager feed plus or minus details into his mind about his people. Dave did this today: good. Harry did that today: bad. He even awards mental points to the performances of the evaluee: three points good for this, five points bad for that. This may sound unlikely, and it is true that no manager actually does this consciously, but sit back and ask yourself if this is not what does go on in your head. You have to have some way of appraising staff during the working day, and this is how you do it – there is no other way.

Now, when we are evaluating people as to their suitability for a job we do it much more consciously and thoroughly, since we are affecting his or her life and our team's success or failure, but the idea is the same. In the next section we look at a simple – and I mean simple – way to evaluate people *on* the job. The headings are different from those which we use to evaluate *for* a job, but the fundamental thought is the same, that a constant appraisal, assessment, rating of your people is absolutely vital if we are to be able to manage them properly.

As far as our five hopefuls are concerned, it is of course of no importance which one was actually picked for the job, since the exercise itself was what we needed. In this case as in all the cases in this book, the important thing was not the decision we arrived at, *it was the road we travelled to arrive at that decision*. We have, all through the book, been exercising our intellects on the sort of problems which we and all managers face every day.

However, while in this case the exercise of choosing was much more important than the choice, there is no need for me to make a mystery out of it. The choice was Bill Benson, the somewhat unexciting, forty-one year old ex canned-goods salesman, and it is worthwhile to pause and ask ourselves: why? As I have said, this case is true, with only enough details altered to disguise the participants, and I was a part of that selection team. Bill Benson was not my choice, although he was high on my list; I wanted Dawn Drake because I thought I had discovered in her a spark which as the trainer in that company I could fan into a bright fire. Who knows, now? I could very well have been wrong.

Anyway, we ask again: why Bill Benson? Well, perhaps a few things. First, he was the only one of the five who had sold copiers, and he did therefore know something of the marketplace for that industry. All things being equal, I have always given the salesman who did *not* know the industry the nod, rather than one who came to me with other people's ideas about a certain type of product line; I prefer to instil my own ideas into him. This would not be a turn-down for me, merely a preference. Then, because of his knowledge of the industry it is possible that his training period could be shortened, and if there was an urgency about putting him into the field then this could be a plus on his side.

Lastly, since management has been defined as a continuous assessment of *risk*, then if you think about it, Bill Benson was probably the low-risk candidate. Probably not an inspired salesman, but then, probably not a born loser, either.

We all carry this mental set of scales around in our heads, don't we? Yes, we do. Whenever we are assessing things, courses of action, or people we put plusses in one side of the scale and minusses in the other side. We do this all the time; we can't help doing it. You might like to go back and do this consciously for the five, and who knows? You may find that Bill is the one who comes up with either the most plusses, or the fewest minusses, and perhaps the minusses are more important.

I did give you a hint, you know. I told you that the assessment after one year was: 'It seems that we made a *reasonable* choice.' The *reasonable* choice was probably Bill.

16

Would you hire him today?

Somewhere between the daily, automatic and almost unconscious rating of your people and the formal, six- or twelve-monthly Appraisal system which your company insists on, there is a gap. Now that I have written that sentence I realise that someone who reads it could be left saying: 'What formal, six- or twelve-monthly Appraisal system?' So let us spend a moment in answering that question.

I have spent too many hours of my life pussy-footing around this subject and I am not going to do it any longer; I am coming right out with it. The truth is that if your company does not have a formal, working appraisal system which involves every single staff member from the top to the bottom then your company is in deep trouble. If you don't have it, or if you have it and its implementation is not strictly enforced then some or all of the following things are happening right now:

- You are losing good people because their merit is not being recognised.

- You have people who are successfully hiding the fact that they are doing a half-day job and getting a full-day's pay.

- You are looking outside the company for someone to fill a key post and all the time there is a staff member sitting three doors down the passage who would be ideal for the job.

- Someone is going crazy trying to do the work of three people.

- A lower-middle manager is causing a communication block; there are problems in his group that you are unaware of which are about to blow up in your face.

- Someone in an obscure department has an idea which could save the company thousands of pounds, but you will never hear about it because he is too shy to come forward.

That sort of thing. If you don't have an appraisal system and you have no idea of how to go about setting one up then there are writings available to you. However, it is probably not necessary to go outside your own organisation; I bet that if you go to one of the long-term people in management and ask about it you will be told: 'Oh, yes; we did have that but we threw it out because it didn't work.'

They threw it out because it didn't work? So bring it back and *make* it work, and a lot of management problems will - no, they will not disappear, but they will become *manageable*.

Enough of that and now let us go back to the start of this section:

Somewhere between the daily, automatic and

almost unconscious rating of your people and the formal, six- or twelve-monthly Appraisal system which your company insists on, there is a gap. The daily plusses and minusses which you put in your mental scales are too arbitrary and short-lived, and the formal appraisals are too far apart from each other – too much can happen in half a year.

So you need something to fill the gap, and if you don't have anything of your own you may care to borrow my idea. I used this when I was in charge of working groups of one sort or another.

If this idea has a strength it is its simplicity. It is such a temptation to make a three-volume compendium when doing something like this, but if you do decide to go ahead with it (and if you do you will have to change the headings to suit your needs) then for goodness' sake keep it *simple*.

You can use this idea or not, as you please; that is your privilege. But if you turn it down don't whatever you do reject it on the ground that it is too elementary. It is *supposed* to be elementary, basic, plain, fundamental, unadorned, naked. Your formal appraisal system has all the goodies, subtleties and ornamentation that you could possibly want; this one is *simple*. It will take you only five minutes for each employee each month, and it will give you a continuous picture of what that person is worth to you, where he is good and where he needs correction.

To me the most important point is the very last one: Would you hire him today? Sit back now and think of one member of your staff. Only one, mind; you can't think of all of them at the same time. Knowing what you do about his performance and his attitude, if he walked in and applied for the job today, would you

NAME ....   DATE ....

DATE OF LAST REVIEW ....

Job Performance
Quantity, quality, economy of operation, other.

−3	−2	−1	0	+1	+2	+3

Job Knowledge
Procedures, regulations, authority and responsibility limits, other.

−3	−2	−1	0	+1	+2	+3

Self-organisation
Work planning, neatness, time control, other.

−3	−2	−1	0	+1	+2	+3

Self-motivation
Initiative, personal goals, ambition, other.

−3	−2	−1	0	+1	+2	+3

Co-operation
Work relationships, compliance, conformity, other.

−3	−2	−1	0	+1	+2	+3

Presence
Personality, appearance, other.

−3	−2	−1	0	+1	+2	+3

Communication
Expression, fluency, persuasiveness, other.

−3	−2	−1	0	+1	+2	+3

Attitude
Towards management, company, job, other.

−3	−2	−1	0	+1	+2	+3

TOTAL RATING:...............Improvement/Deterioration since last review?

Would you hire this employee today? Yes/No

hire him? On balance, you would? Go on to the next one. Same question. And the next. Same question. And the next.

Suppose, when you have added the plus points and the minus points for a particular person, that you have a minus total. Does that mean that you would *not* hire him today? Well, probably it does. But, and this is a big but, does it mean that you are going to call him in this afternoon and fire him? Certainly not. You are going to call him in, lay out his sins of omission and commission, tell him that in spite of these he is well worth saving, and put on paper a timetable of salvation. Then you and he are committed to improving his performance until the plus points far outweigh the minus points and he is on the road to glory – or until it has been proved beyond all doubt that he cannot be snatched from the burning.

That would make a case history worthy of being recorded alongside the others in this book, would it not?

17

This is a manager

A manager is someone who manages people.

In these pages we have observed, examined and analysed managers managing people. We have seen them succeed and fail in their dealings with people. They have succeeded because of empathy, patience, knowledge, restraint and courage; they have failed because of inexperience, ignorance, intolerance, fear or simply because circumstances were too much against them.

Since no person is identical to another person and since no people problems exactly duplicate other people problems, you naturally understand that you cannot lift the words and actions found in these cases and use them in your management situations in precisely the way they were used here. In any case, you have your own unique management style and you deal with people and situations as that style dictates, adapting it to suit each specific circumstance and condition. However, if the cases have helped you to gain a deeper insight into why people do things and how they react to certain stimuli – or even if they have simply allowed you to exercise your skills in management – then part of the objective of this book has been attained.

The other objective if you remember was to set it out in such a way that you found it absorbing, interesting and even exciting.

You must be the judge of that.

Index